God's Blue Book

— *Love God, Love One Another* —

Volume 3

Messages received by
Rita Ring

Shepherds of Christ Publications
P.O. Box 193
Morrow, Ohio 45152

In conformity with the decrees of Pope Urban VIII, the Publisher recognizes and accepts that the final authority regarding all messages rests with the Holy See of Rome, to whose judgment we willingly submit.

—The Publisher

This book is published by Shepherds of Christ Publications, a subsidiary of Shepherds of Christ Ministries, a tax exempt, religious public charitable association.

For additional copies, write to:
Shepherds of Christ Publications
P.O. Box 193
Morrow, Ohio 45152

First Printing: August, 1996
Second Printing: March, 1997
Third Printing: August, 1998

About the cover:
"I love each of you dearly. I write this letter to you this day. Read every letter as My love letter to you. Read the letters as you would from someone you love. Open your heart to every word I write to you. You are My beloved loved ones. Look at My picture as I talk to you."

—Message from Jesus

This is the picture I want in My messages. When you read these messages, look at My picture and know I love you. These messages are My words of love for each of you.

Dedication

To Father Carter

Acknowledgements

For his gracious assistance in discerning this text and for helping me on my spiritual journey, I extend my heartfelt appreciation to Father Edward J. Carter, S.J., Professor of Theology, Xavier University, Cincinnati, Ohio.

A great many people have given unselfishly of their time and talents to make this book possible but a certain few stand out for their special contributions. They have been there from early on and continue to be there whenever help is needed: Ellen Sartori for typing these messages and for giving of herself for those seemingly endless hours of service to Jesus and my uncle Andrew Weber, who has been so strongly supportive.

—*RR*

CONTENTS

To The Reader

Jesus wants to share His love with you. He comes in these letters to tell you how you can be in intimate union with Him.

All of us possess everything we need to have an intimate union with Him. He has been giving me messages since October of 1991. For at least a year I sat in front of the tabernacle and begged him to talk to me. I wanted words. I prayed to the Holy Spirit and begged and begged Him to baptize me. After a long and seemingly endless search, trying to hear God, He told me to "feed the hungry." For six weeks this was all I heard. I thought maybe I wasn't feeding my children well or eating well enough myself. What a long wait for three words! At long last one day, as I was writing to Jesus, I received a letter back. He told me, "I am Jesus, Son of the Living God." I did not want to write this but it kept coming—and so did many other messages. I knew nothing of anyone getting messages. I wrote them, reluctantly, and hid my notebooks. The letters kept coming, many during the night. I would be awakened, then given long letters which I felt compelled to get up and write down. I read these letters privately and my life began to change. I felt a new life within me.

He taught me of His fervent love and how truly present He was. He taught me how precious I was to Him. Over and over again He would call me His precious child and tell me how He loved me, how He clothed me with dignity and honor. He told me over and over how He was right by my side always. He is teaching me to give up all fear and to trust in Him. He is teaching me to let go of myself and let Him run my life. I am trying every day to do His will.

He is also telling you in your heart all you need to know. He has all the answers for you there in your heart. You must be silent and go to Him so you can hear His words for you.

Sit in front of the tabernacle and be with Him. Do not pray prayers. Sit and be open and just be with Him. Read these letters there. These are Jesus' love letters to you. Sit in front of the tabernacle and let Him talk to you. Sit silent awhile. Read these letters part of the time. Open any page and He will talk to you. Do not read this like a book, cover to cover. Just open to a page and read that page. That is the way He speaks to you.

Introduction*

*Words of Jesus. Read before the Tabernacle.

How, child, do I, Jesus, tell you I love you? You hold on to silly things when God is in your midst and is ardently loving you. I am Jesus Christ, the Son of God. I am writing to each precious child this day. I am on fire for love of you. I remain in the Eucharist to be with you with My ardent love. I did not want to leave My beloved ones at the Last Supper. I love you so, My dear and ardently loved children. I remain with you this day in the Blessed Sacrament, the same Jesus Who died a brutal death on the Cross.

Do you know I am truly present there? Do you know that God waits every day for you in the tabernacle? Do you comprehend even a minute amount of My love?

I, Jesus, truly the Son of God, came to earth a man and suffered a brutal death for love of you. I love you so much! I remain with you this day. I long for your love. I want you to come and be with Me in front of the tabernacle. I wait, I yearn for you to come and whisper your love to Me. I am a Person and I love you this day, with such an ardent on-fire love! No human could ever compare a speck to My love for you.

I wait, little ones, in the tabernacle. I wait for you to come and receive Me in Communion. I want you to want Me so much you cannot wait to come and receive Me. I want to be the love, the center of your life!

I am Jesus. I am the Son of God. I am writing to you this day. I want to possess your very soul and live in you. I have all you need, sweet ones. Oh, you are so blind! I long for your union with Me. I wrote the book of love. I instituted it, yet you go to the world for your love and do not even come to Me! Oh, I love you, little ones. Little ones, beloved of the Father, loved by the Holy Spirit, mothered by My very own mother! What more can I say? The rest is up to you!

I give you your will with such love and I want your love freely given. I am God. What do you think you could ever need that I do not give you? I am the Savior of this world. I am Jesus, the Son of God. I am waiting for you. I am longing for you. I am yearning for you. I am God. I have all you ever will need!

Surrender this life to Me. Pray My Prayer for Union with Me. I want to possess your soul and operate from your very being. I am Jesus. I am the Son of God. I am the Sacred Heart of Jesus. I am Who am. I died and rose on the third day.

Harken to My call, harken to My pleading. Spend your days in love with Me. Nothing matters unless it is rooted in Me and rooted in My love. I am the Son of God. I am the Sacred Heart of Jesus. I love you with the tenderest love. I am waiting this day for just you, My beloved one. Come to Me for I am the tenderest of all hearts. I am the Sacred Heart of Jesus.

— God's Blue Book, Volume 2
April 13, 1994

Prayer for Union With Jesus

Come to me, Lord, and possess my soul. Come into my heart and permeate my soul. Help me to sit in silence with You and let You work in my heart.

I am Yours to possess. I am Yours to use. I want to be selfless and only exist in You. Help me to spoon out all that is me and be an empty vessel ready to be filled by You. Help me to die to myself and live only for You. Use me as You will. Let me never draw my attention back to myself. I only want to operate as You do, dwelling within me.

I am Yours, Lord. I want to have my life in You. I want to do the will of the Father. Give me the strength to put aside the world and let You operate my very being. Help me to act as You desire. Strengthen me against the distractions of the devil to take me from Your work.

When I worry, I have taken my focus off of You and placed it on myself. Help me not to give in to the promptings of others to change what in my heart You are making very clear to me. I worship You, I adore You and I love You. Come and dwell in me now.

January 17, 1994

This prayer originally appeared in God's Blue Book Number 1. By reciting it each time the book is opened, the reader asks the intercession of Jesus, not just for deeper understanding of the messages, but for closer union with Him every moment of our lives as well. This prayer should be prayed often—many times each day if possible—out of love for and consecration to His Sacred Heart.
—R.R.

It is in acceptance of all that is before you that you grow in your relationship with Me. Do not try to throw back the opportunity for grace you receive.

Child, I am ever by your side and I am ever teaching you. I am vigilant and by your side. Nothing happens to you that I have not consented to.

— Jesus' words to Rita
December 30, 1993

The Sharing of Love
—More Dialogues With Jesus—

As in Volumes 1 and 2, most messages in this book are from Jesus to the receiver. Some are from Our Lady. For clarity, the receiver's words are always preceded by the letter **R.**, indented more severely, vertically marked by a thin continuation line and visually separated from Jesus' words by extra vertical white text space. Where confusion might otherwise result, notations preceding certain text identify the speaker in italics.

— The Editor

April 1, 1994 Good Friday   **5:15a.m.**

My Messages Must Circulate

My little one, be wrapped in My arms. I am Jesus and I am truly here. You never walk alone. I want you to let go. Just let go of all that is troubling you. I am with you and I am God.

You don't have to explain these letters to any man. You write as I dictate to you. You are My hands to write these letters. Know, sweet one, that I am with you in all these trials. I know your sufferings and I comfort you.

You will be tried, you will be tested, you will be persecuted. Stay rooted in My love. Do not give in to Satan to get you off your course. I am ever guarding you. Doubt, worry and anxiety are from Satan. Remember how quickly he can get you focused on a problem. Do not think. Turn it immediately to Me. Forgive your brother. Do not feel attached.

Look at Me hanging on the cross. My blood was spent. I did this for love of you. Do you not think I am guarding you at this very moment? I am Jesus Christ, the Son of the Living God. I am here, My beloved daughter.

I am Jesus, child. Nothing else matters. I talk to you and you worry or fret. I have all the power. I am talking to you. Do not give in to Satan. He wants this book stopped. He will go to any lengths to stop it. It will truly turn the cold hearts to Me. My words are so powerful! No man can say what God has said to you in these pages!

I will triumph in the end. I will give them all they need to accomplish My tasks. Tell them to quit doubting. I am Jesus and I talk to them. The doubt they have is harmful to production of this book.

1

They need to sit in front of the tabernacle. I am pleased with their efforts to do this.

Pray to know My Will. I want My letters published. Soon is not soon enough. I will provide everything to get this accomplished. I am Jesus. I am God. Do you not know I have all the power? Satan is working to divide you. Be assured he will attack you all through each other and those closest to you. Stay steadfast in My love. You have such an important work to do together. You must stay united. Do not listen to Satan in your head to get you to doubt this work or one another. You all operate from love of Me.

Come and sit in front of the tabernacle. Let no man distract you—ever—or stop your time with Me. This is your food for your soul every day. Tell them to leave. Do whatever you have to do, but one solid, uninterrupted hour with Me will give you what you need!

Choose this time before you eat. This is most important. Do not let others distract you. Take your thoughts to Me and dismiss them. I will tell you in your heart all you need to know. Have faith. Pray for all you need to do My work. Make yourself like jello. You are formless. I form you into what you need to be.

I am Jesus, I talk to you. You must be aware that Satan comes in sheep's clothing. He will do anything to stop this book. Has he not already? I Jesus, the Son of God, beg you to listen to Me. My children are sick and need this medicine now. Give them their medicine. I will be with you in all things.

Sit and I will bring you all you need. You think you must do things. Your doing things you think you ought to do is botching things up! Wait on Me! I will bring you all you need. A choir of angels surrounds you and you are never alone. I and My Blessed Mother go with you where you go.

I want this work accomplished. I have all the power. I will see to its production. I want you to continue steadfastly putting out My words of love. Souls will be turned to Me and fed by these letters. They are starving. You are providing them with their food. Oh, how I loved them to My death! I loved each one of you individually. I want them to read My letters. Tell them of My ardent, personal love. Oh, I love them.

My hand writes here these beautiful letters to My beloved ones. I ask you to deliver My words of love to My little ones. Thank you for your work for Me. You are My beloved servants. You I love. You I guard. You I protect. Turn to Me and know I am present with you all at this very moment! I am counting on you, My beloved ones, with a Heart on fire for love of you.

R. (I feel His presence and His love. He is truly here with me.) Oh, Jesus, my beloved, how I love You, how I lament Your torture this night (Holy Thursday). I cry out to You, beloved of Your love.

When I speak, they listen. They are dying of starvation. They want to be fed.

R. Jesus, Jesus, who am I that You write to me?

I am the messenger. They (the messages) are hand-delivered to you from Him Who loves you. You are His favored ones. Each child He clothes in honor and dignity. Each child is precious to Him. Each child He loves uniquely and bids come to Him. He loves you this very day. He would die this very day for you and you alone. Hear Him. He speaks to you!

Please continue to publish My Blue Book #2. I want My letters to reach all the hurting hearts. You are all chosen. You have been primed. You I will sustain and make strong! Come and be with Me. I am Jesus Christ. I hold you up, I love you dearly, I protect you and care for you. You are My beloved ones.

Come and lay yourselves in My arms. I am waiting to caress and hold you. Put all doubt aside and feel My firm hold. No fear will befall you for I am holding you in My arms. Surrender to Me. Let go. Let Me run your life. Come and be with Me, My beloved ones. I wait for you in the tabernacle.

I am Jesus, the Son of God, and I wait for you, My precious ones. I love you!

April 1, 1994   **10:00a.m.**

I Gave My Life for You

When you are troubled in thought, turn all your thoughts to Me. Focus on Me and My love for you. I, God, loved you so much that I suffered this brutal walk on Calvary and a horrid, brutal, suffering death. I loved you to My death. I love you, little ones.

R. I must focus on Jesus. If I begin to worry, I must think of His dying on the cross for love of me. I love Him so and want to serve Him.

The more I can make Him the focus of My life, the more I will act as He wants me to. I must see all my thoughts as thoughts that will render service to His love.

When I see my brothers, I must see them as Jesus, Who lives in them. If I see Jesus first, then I will not want to judge them or criticize them, but love them. I love Jesus. They are His most precious beloved ones, even if they are in darkness.

They all are brothers, His precious, loving children. If one member of my family were sick, I would love them more. He asks us to see them all as our brothers. We are all members in Christ's family. I must love my brothers who are hurting. I must act as He wants me to, to see them as my brothers in Christ, to see Christ first. To approach every person with love is His way.

He loves us all in our darkest sin. He loves us unconditionally. He tells us to love one another. I love my brothers, nice or not nice. But this is hard to do. I can only love as Jesus if I am totally in union with Him. I stay in union with Him after Communion and in front of the tabernacle. He gives me His love in abundance there. I am charged as a battery, charged with the love of God!

This is My call: to love God and love one another. Love is action from your heart. When you operate, keep Me always in front of you, Me and My immense love for you! My love never wears out. There is never a shortage. I fill you to the brim. You come from a place of being loved and feeling good and you can give love to all of your brothers.

You are brothers in Me. I died for each and every soul. I want to save each and every person. I loved each and every person to My death. I walked the walk and My thoughts were for you. I thought of you and I endured such horridness out of My ardent love. Will you not love My beloved ones for Me?

You are My heart to this cold world. You will warm this cold world with My heart filled with love for all. Love My beloved ones for Me. Love every one of your brothers. Focus on Me first. Do not see their weaknesses. See only My great love for them. Trust them as your beloved brothers, hurting or not, and love them. You are My heart, you are My hands, you are My voice. You speak My love. Do not ever speak words of hate to My beloved ones. To My death I loved them and loved you. What you do to your brothers you do to Me. See Me, love Me in your brothers. This is My commandment: love God and love one another.

I showed you the way. I gave My life for you. I loved those who persecuted Me and beat Me. Love is the only way. Focus on Me, My child, focus on Me. In your every thought, let all your actions flow only as they serve Me. Focus on Me first when you see your brothers. You are being taught by God Himself. This is My way. I loved you to My death. Can you not love My hurting ones for Me?

April 2, 1994   5:15a.m.
I Am Present in the Eucharist

My child, you come in the night. I give you a message for this world. I am Jesus, Son of the Living God. My beloved ones are hurting from all the evil in this world. I want you to preach of My love. I want you to tell all how I am truly present and I am waiting for My little ones to come to Me.

Preach the True Presence. Talk about Jesus Christ, the Son of God, and how He is alive and in the Eucharist and waiting in the tabernacle. Tell all Catholics or other faiths that the priest has the power to change bread and wine into My Body and My Blood.

Many Catholics do not realize that I, Jesus Christ, the Son of God, am present in the Eucharist. They come to My altar and receive Me and do not even think of Me. How this wounds My aching Heart. Tell priests to talk about the Eucharist and how Jesus, the Son of God, is truly present there.

I am God. I have all the healing any soul ever needs. If people come to Me, if they receive Me in Holy Communion, they are receiving God, fully present, into their breasts. Tell them to come with such reverence and devotion. Tell them to come with their hearts on fire. Tell them to receive Me and know that I am truly Jesus, the Son of God. Nothing can be more healing than receiving God in your breast. Nothing you ever do will compare to this union with God.

Tell all how I, Jesus, the Son of God, am truly present. I quiet their fears and I fill them with My peace. I know them far more than they know themselves. Come to Me, My little, beloved ones. Come and receive your God. Nothing you do all day can compare to receiving the Son of God inside of your breast. I am the bread of life. I feed you with My very own flesh and blood. I nourish you. I give you all you need. Nothing on the face of this earth can compare to My presence.

Come and let go of all your cares. Do not fret or fume as to what you are to wear or eat or do, or how you will live. Come and give Me yourself. I take care of all the birds of the air and lilies of the field. You, who are so much more precious—I come and I take care of you!

Give Me yourself. Spend time with Me. Surrender all that is dear to you. You, child, are receiving the one, true God. I await you with love, not condemnation. I await you with My arms open wide. I wait for you to come and be so close to Me.

Do not come bowed down. Satan constantly tells you you are not good enough. I look on you with such love! I await your union with Me.

You are a sinner. You make mistakes. You do not love when you can love. You do not obey and you do your own will constantly. You are ignorant. You do not even know how you choose selfish ways over loving ways. Say you are sorry at the beginning of Mass. Say you are sorry before you receive Me. Try to see how you can love your brothers more. Then, when you receive Me, forget your unworthiness and focus on My love. I can heal you, My sweet ones. I am God and I am truly present in the Eucharist. I give Myself to you in Holy Communion out of ardent love for you. If I, God, come to you with such love, do you not think I will shower you with My gifts when you come with your love and reverence?

Please, My children, think of My True Presence! Realize that I am God and I am coming and dwelling inside of you. Give Me all your cares. Come and give Me all your love. I am a real Person. I am truly present, Body and Blood, Soul and Divinity, in the meal you receive there.

Do not be busy for your earthly food. Feed your soul with manna from heaven. Fill your hearts with the presence of the Divine God. Oh, children, how do I get you to realize this is all you need? Come to Me every day. Do not ever miss a day when you could receive Me. This is more important than anything you do on this earth. This is more important than your food or your sleep. Little ones, you receive the Son of God there!

Oh, please open your eyes. Please preach My presence. Please tell all what a miracle you possess in the Eucharist. Tell all of My ardent, on-fire love for each child individually. Never miss an opportunity to receive Me.

I am Jesus, Son of God. The gift I give you is Myself. Come and receive Me, the Divine Healer, and ask for your healing. Come and give Me homage. Come and receive the one, true, magnificent God. Come one, come all. I love you each so uniquely with this ardent love. I await you this very day. I have all you need. Bring all your children to Me. Let your children know I am God and I am truly present in the Eucharist. Take them to Communion. Watch miracles happen in your life. Read the children these letters. Teach them young about My ardent love. This is the greatest gift you can give your beautiful children. Tell them how Jesus, the Son of God, awaits and loves them in the Eucharist.

Tell them what love I have for them. Teach the parents. Tell them to tell the very young how God is truly there waiting for them. Oh, what a gift for your child! Does any gift even come close to the gift of God Himself?

When you enkindle a love affair with Me, you will know that the things of this world are so empty. Nothing compares to the love of God. Nothing you buy or eat or do is even the tiniest comparison to Me. The more you enkindle this love affair with Me, the less other things will be important to you.

I am the Son of God. I come to you. Come and worship Me and be fed! The more you come to Me, the more you will realize that nothing compares to God inside you.

You develop your love affair with Me and I will tend to your life. You are drawn to Me like steel to a magnet. This magnetic attraction keeps you coming back. The soul is only fed by the love of God. My little dear ones, I have all you need. Do you not see the folly in your ways? Do you not feel all you receive when you come to Me? You want Me more, you seek Me more, you do not satisfy any part of your soul, with anything but God! All the roads you wander to receive such momentary gratification and you are left empty. I feed your starving soul. I am God. Nothing even comes close to Me.

I love you dearly. I am your ardent lover. I await you. I long for your love. I am alive. I am in your midst and I come to you in the Eucharist.

R.Alleluia. God has come in their midst and has showered each heart with His abundant love.

April 2, 1994

He Acts Through Me

R.Oh, God, this is my ardent plea to You: to become selfless and only exist for the love of You; to know, love and serve You. This is my goal, this is my struggle: to empty out myself and live as You want me to live.

Of myself, Lord, I cannot do this task. I can only do this as You possess me, as You give me all I need to do this. I am willing, Lord. You are my Savior. Operate me and take me to Yourself. Use me to do Your work. I am Yours, Lord. I love You so.

Alleluia. The night was over, the battle won. He rose victorious on the third day and we watched with awe because He is truly God and we are but mere mortals. He is our Savior. We are His beloved ones. He is God. We are merely human, but He chose to give of Himself for love of us. Oh, how is it that we are favored so?

Oh, He is God. He has won the victory and we are His grateful heirs. Oh, Jesus, oh, Jesus, we worship and honor and adore You! You are our victory. You are truly the one, true, magnificent God. Alleluia. Alleluia.

I see now how He has His hand in our lives. We, in our foolishness, think we accomplish such great things. He is constantly molding and shaping us for His work and His kingdom. We look to ourselves and see a job well done, only to look over our lives and see His hand in everything we accomplished. To see how He so lovingly taught us lessons and teaches us today! He is forever with us with such love! Look to our past and see Him teaching us lessons that brought us closer to Him and His work for us.

What does He ask me today? All the years of my blindness, my worry, my frets, my control, my reliance on myself, only to realize that He has been truly by my side at every step. When I was down, His loving eyes were looking into mine and comforting me. When I was high, and taking the glory, His eyes beheld me still, with love.

Oh, sweet surrender, Lord, to the self that wants to reign and is so incapable. Without You, Lord, I cannot love like you. Without you, Lord, I cannot do anything. I surrender this willful self to You and ask You to possess my soul. Help me to die to me, only to live in You.

April 3, 1994 Easter Sunday

I Love You—You Love Your Brothers

My child, calm yourself. Live only for love of Me. Live for Me and Me alone. You love Me and I love you. Your love for others will flow from your love for Me. I sustain you. I give you everything you need. Your life is but a breath here. Do not ever focus on it. Remain selfless. Rid yourself constantly of self and operate only to know, love and serve Me.

I am Jesus, the Son of God. Oh, little one, such love I have for you. Do you even know? This is not a myth. This is real. I am real. The unseen world is real. It is your faith that will sustain you. I am Jesus, the Son of God, Rita. God is talking to you. You have a job to do for all My beloved ones. I love them so. I want you to tell them of My deep and ardent love. Surrender yourself into the arms of Him Who sustains you. I catch you. I cuddle you and you, child are not suspended in mid-air. You are held tight by the hands of God. I showed you the way, child. I let go on the cross. Life comes only in this surrendering. I let go, I died that I might rise again on Easter!

You die to yourself that you will live in My love. You will rise victorious in the love of Jesus. Oh, child, I am so real and I love you. What can I do to tell you how I do love you!

Live in My love. Do not judge. Do not spend idle time making yourself better than your brother. Think only of Me and how I love you. You have your job: (1) to love Me with all your heart and (2) to love your brother as yourself. Do not look on your brother with anything but love. How freeing! Love finds a way! Where hate keep you tied to yourselves, loving one and all frees you. Love Me. Love your brothers. They are responsible for their lives. You are responsible for your life.

Your job is to love. I call you, My little ones, to love of Me and love of one another. You will answer according to how you loved. You will not be judged on the amount of money you made, on your worldly possessions, on your clean rugs, on your affairs in order. You will answer for how you loved Me and loved your fellow men. You cannot love and remain selfish. Love gives to the other, love is rendering, love in no way demands itself.

The world tells you to think of yourself, give yourself pleasure, marry for your self-fulfillment, look out for yourself.The world is focused on self. I tell you that you will be judged on how you loved. Love gives of self. Love is rendering. Love does not demand its way. Love gives to the other. How can marriage work when people are living for themselves. You cannot love and be selfish at the same time. Love does not demand its own way. Love does not seek itself. Love is as I showed you when I died on the cross. I gave My all for love of you, in total surrender.

I call you, little ones, to this love. You say, "Oh, is this what you demand?" I say, "Unless you die to yourself, you will not have My life within you." Love never demands its own way. I call you to love of God, love of one another! I showed you the way. I give you all you need to follow My way. You must give Me your life. When you become selfless, you are filled by the love and life of Christ.

The life I give is a power so mighty it cannot be contained. It is emitted from your being. You love and live in Me in your being when you strip yourself of yourself.

I ask you now to surrender your thoughts, thoughts that constantly go on in your head to make you better than your brothers! Focus on Me and how I love you. Focus on how I am truly alive this day and in your midst and I want to dwell in you in love. Focus on Me. Rid yourself of yourself. Look at every person with love. Do not look with any competition or making yourself better than them. You have your job to do, they have theirs. You are all uniquely created.

Each person is perfect and loved dearly by Me. I love your brothers with My Sacred Heart. Love them as I do. I love you in all your weaknesses, in all your flaws. I love you dearly. I do not count your sins. I love you with an ardent love. I love your brothers. I, God, love all your brothers the way I love you.

Who are you to look on your brother with thoughts of "he is wrong, I am right"? You are loved so immensely by Me and My Father and the Holy Spirit and the Blessed Lady. You are surrounded by this love! You need not the approval or love of your brother. You need to give love to them! You can do this when you come and sit with Me in front of the tabernacle and after communion. You can do this when you surrender yourselves and live only for love of Me and love of them.

You are learning, child. Loving one another is freeing. You are not attached. You are free. You are not attached to your brother and how he responds to you. You love only from the love of God. You are attached to My love and My love never flickers or goes away. My love is always there. I am madly in love with you. Forgive your brother when he is cruel. Love him as I do. Come to Me for your love. I have all you need. Oh, child, you are being taught mighty lessons. The ways of God are so simple, but they are the only way. When you free yourself of your attachments to how others treat you, you will know such mental freedom.

You preach My lessons of love in how you model yourself after Me. Love the unloving and preach the message of love. You are My heart in the cold world. I am your lover. You can love because I have loved you first. I love you with a Heart on fire! Come and let Me give you this love this very day! You will love your brothers if you focus on Me. My way is the only way. My way is love!

April 3, 1994 Easter Sunday
I Have Risen To Give New Life

R.Jesus told me on Easter morning to go to a church I had never attended. Jesus was not in the church. They had a table for the altar. The tabernacle was in the corner. There was no sanctuary light. I asked a sister if Jesus was there. She took some hosts out of the freezer in a refrigerator. They were in a baggie. She put them in a bowl in the tabernacle. There was still no light. They had a policeman to direct traffic. People walked in front of the tabernacle in the corner and paid no heed to Jesus. The chairs had their backs to the tabernacle.

Who is this, our Savior, Jesus, the Son of God? God is here, mightier than any king. He is God! Who even pays Him homage? He told me to kiss the floor. I left and cried. This, my people, is the Son of God. They are hurting. They are coming to be fed. I have personal letters from Jesus declaring His love for them. Oh, Jesus, I want to spread your love! I love You so!

Jesus, I am so sorry for all the neglect and indifference. Please send us holy priests to spread Your love. Help me to circulate Your love letters. On this Easter, I vow to do all You lead me to do to spread the ardent on-fire love of Jesus. Use me, fashion me. I want to tell the world how You are in our midst this very day and how You love each of us so much.

Lip service: "the love of God"?? He loved *us* to His death and resurrection. New life for this world! Jesus, Jesus, I consecrate my life to You and Your most Sacred Heart.

My little sweet one, no matter what you do, love for Me. Do not get bowed down, but shed My light to this dark world. Love, My sweet one. Do not argue. Do not defend yourself. Come and be in My Presence. I love you. I guard you. I watch over you. You are My beloved.

This, child, is the Easter message for you and all My beloved ones. Share this with all: "I have risen to give new life. Give My life to all those around you. Love My beloved ones for Me."

R.Alleluia. And He came and gave us strength to do the work He calls us to do, to love a dark world, one that is hurting.

I am the Way. I am the Truth. I am the Life. Alleluia.

In Suffering We Gain Life

It is in your suffering that you are given life. It was through My suffering and death that I rose on the third day. You suffer and you have been raised up with your life in Me. It is in the cross that you are given My life. Your love for Me developed from much suffering.

You are given suffering. Die to your self and be alive in Me. I died that you might live. Die to yourself! Do not ever hate. Do not make your brother wrong or right. Have faith in Me and Me alone that you might live!

You are human. You suffer. You say things. Say you are sorry and be loving. It is in your humbleness to be sorry that I forgive you.

April 4, 1994   1:00a.m.
He Loves Us Just As We Are

Dear child, let go. You are far from perfect. I love you just as you are. You will fight an uphill battle. Others will not know where you are coming from. You must continue to love the blind. They are hurting and in need of My love. Do not get angered. You must remain calm. You will be attacked constantly. Satan wants to stop you. Focus on My love for you. Focus on how close you are to Me and how you love Me. This is all there is: love of God, love of one another.

The world wants you like the world. They want you centered on incidentals. You see with different eyes. All of this is of no account unless it has reference to Me. All of this will pass soon. Others are attached. They do not even see that this life is not the end. You must teach this. Your job is to talk, child. Do not shy away. See their blindness and respond with love. You, child, have a message from Jesus Christ, the Son of God. They do not want to listen because they do not want to give up their world. Keep talking as I prompt you to.

You have a message to save your brother's soul. They are hurting, even in their arrogance. They need My words. You must constantly pray for My beloved ones. Offer up your sacrifices. The world is only a layover. You have a big job to do for Me. Focus on Me and My love. You must deliver My message or no one will hear!

Love My beloved ones for Me, My child. I need you strong. I am Jesus Christ and I have chosen you to deliver My messages. You must speak. Satan wants you bowed down.

I am the Alpha. I am the Omega. I am God. I have used you. I will use you. Sit tight. Let others move about and bump their heads. You pray for them and I will deliver all you need. Your music was easy, was it not, when you let go? I did all you needed to do.

I am God and I need you to deliver messages about My love. Every person can have an intimate on-fire relationship with Me. They are being stopped by their own choosing. I am Jesus Christ. I am God and I, God, speak to you here, child. Never feel bowed down. Focus on this great gift. I love you so, little one. I love you. I love you. I love you. That is all you need to know!

April 4, 1994   After Mass
Dismiss All Hate and Anger

You must dismiss all hate and anger. Empty yourself totally to My love. Focus on love of Me and love of your brothers. They are hurting. They act as they do because they are suffering.

A heart of God only loves. Practice silence when others say things you do not like. Say, "Jesus, Jesus," and turn it over to Me. I am with you, little one. I never leave you. You have such lessons to learn about love. You must dismiss your thoughts. Satan works in your thoughts. He tells you to defend yourself. You must die to self and live only for love of Me. Pray the Prayer for Union with Jesus. You must beg to be selfless. The self is constantly wanting its way. It wants to defend itself, it wants to be right. You only operate from love. Beg to be freed of your self.

I will take care of you. Open yourself up to Me and let Me possess your soul. I am here at this moment. I never leave you. You are feeling alone. You are never alone. I am with you at every second. Quit focusing on yourself and your doing it. Let go, let Me operate you. You have nothing to fear.

I am God. I have all the power. I will triumph in the end. Let go, child, let go and fall into My waiting arms. I sustain you. I cuddle you. I hold you up. You do not drop into the air. You are upheld by the loving arms of God. What more could you ask for? Oh, how I love you, little one. Surrender to Me. Let Me operate your whole being. You need never fret for anything. I am God, little one. I loved you to My death. Jesus.

April 5, 1994
To Focus on Self Is Satan's Way

The way of Satan is to focus on self. When you are attacked by others, you focus on your self. If you remain selfless, they cannot touch you. Operate only for love of God. I do not demand perfection. Those closest to you are being used by Satan to get to you. If you are criticized, they are trying to focus on what you did wrong.

Take it to Me. I do not tell you that you are wrong. I want you to come to Me. When others focus on you, respond in love. Do not let anyone shame you or make you feel guilty. This is the work of Satan. I never shame you or make you feel guilty. My way is love. I demand love of those who want to serve Me. To love someone, you are giving to the other, not criticizing, not looking for personal gain.

When anyone is criticizing you, telling you that you have wronged them and that you are not any good, this is not from God. The way of God is to love your brother. To take up sides, to make yourself better than your brother, to make him wrong and you right, this is coming from the evil one. My way is love. Love is giving. Love does not seek its own way. Love focuses on bringing the other close to God. The way to Me is the way of love. In all things, love your brothers, be kind, do not look for personal gain. You owe no man an explanation on these letters. You are being persecuted and I am allowing it. You must accept your suffering and focus on your children. I am there with you in your darkest hour. I never leave your side.

Satan wants you to doubt and stop this work. He wants you to focus on yourself and feel sorry for yourself. You must die to all thoughts that make you right and others wrong. This is very hard to do. You must see your brothers with only love. You must never measure them or yourself. You are not better, they are not better. You are all My beloved ones! You are all precious. You were all given special gifts to do exactly the work you will be called to do.

Never shame or blame or criticize your brothers. Pray for them. Be kind when you talk to them. You know the way to Me is the way of the cross. It is hard to love and be kind when you feel hurt. This is what I call you to do: look at Me with My flesh torn and see Me loving My attackers. I answered not one thing back. I was silent. I loved those who beat Me. I showed you the way. The way to Me is the way of love.

Making yourself right and others wrong is from Satan. Cast him out! You must do as I command you to do. You must never want to offend Me. You must keep My commandments. Others can do as they please. Pray for them.

You have such a gift! If others listen to you, they will learn from Me. I am talking directly to you. If they do not listen, they will miss the words given by God to you. Do not force your speech on anyone. They are missing My words if they keep talking. I can say in three words what others can never say. Speak to those who are open. Those who do not want to listen will not hear.

You, My child, are learning to be Christ-like. If others demand perfection of you, they are not coming from Me. I do not demand perfection from any human. I want you to say you are sorry when you have sinned. I want you to strive to be saints. I do not tell you to be perfect. That is Satan who points out your faults! Always love, child. Do not judge. Do not get angry. Pray for My help. You need My constant love. Stay fixed in Me. I love you in your failings. Say you are sorry and go about loving for Me.

I love you. I want a contrite heart. Clean your heart at every second. Your heart is holding on to hurts. I am God and I, Jesus Christ, love you. Do not worry about your struggling brothers. I can give as no human can. Come to Me and let Me fill you. Forget your brothers who are angered at you. Pray for them. They are hurting inside. Respond with love!

Be there for your children. Pray and play with them. This is your test to stay focused on Me and doing My Will. Satan is really working on you. You are suffering persecution. If he stops you, he will have a big victory. Forget others who attack you and play with your precious ones. I love you so much. I am Jesus, the Son of God, child. What more do you want?

April 6, 1994

I Am the Sacred Heart of Jesus

I am the Sacred Heart of Jesus. I am your shield in this dark, cold world. You may wonder about here and wonder what is to come, but I shield you. I lift you up. Come to Me and be filled in your heart. You will not be harmed or led astray if you keep focusing on Me. Come to daily Mass and Communion and sit for long periods with Me, especially after Communion.

You will be tested. You will suffer to live in this world that is so blind, but I am with you. God is with you, My precious child. I never leave you and you never walk alone. Hold on. I need you here to love My precious ones for Me! To die in this world would leave Me with one less mighty soldier to do My work. You are My warrior in this cold war. I need you with your heart full of My love. I am the Sacred Heart of Jesus. I dwell in you and you radiate My presence from your being. I live through you and I minister to My hurting ones. Your job is far from over. Your job is beginning! You stand on the outskirts of the city and you will walk My walk and lead many to My most Sacred Heart.

I am the Sacred Heart of Jesus. I am God. I dwell within your breast. I will operate from you and lead so many to My waiting arms. Do not fume or fret or be anxious in any way. I have not lost any control. My plan is unfolding. Why your anxiousness, when I, God, am in charge? Rita, I will not fail. I will do all I need to. Put all anxiety and unrest aside. Satan is getting to you. My urgency has nothing to do with you. I want My letters out. You keep doing what you are doing. Do not be anxious for I am in charge.

I am God. I will tend to all I need to do. I am the Sacred Heart of Jesus. I am by your side and you waste our precious time being anxious. I want to be close to you and love you. Do not worry, for I am God and My work will be accomplished. I will use you, and time is perfect for My plan. I am the Sacred Heart of Jesus. I am truly present, with My Heart on fire for love of you.

Let go, child, let go, let go! I am ablaze for love of you and every one of My precious children, even those who are in total darkness.

My Heart is on fire for love of them. I am the Sacred Heart of Jesus. I am on fire. I am ablaze. I am Who am and I have all the power. I am the Sacred Heart of Jesus.

Accept Your Crosses

I am Jesus, the Son of God. You do not need to read the little book. Read My letters to you. I talk to you with the same tenderness and love. I am truly present with you at this very moment. I want you to get up in the night. I want to be with you. You will not suffer any loss of sleep. You will be revived. Do not fret or fume. Be at peace in My love. I am tending to your very need. Oh, beloved, when will you let go? Let go, sweet one. I am forever by your side. You are full of such uneasiness. I love you so much. Let go, sweet one. Jesus, the Son of God, is with you and He loves you.

I am the Way. I am the Truth. I am the Life. He that abides in Me will have eternal life. I am truly present in all the tabernacles of this world. Jesus Christ, the Son of God is in your midst and who pays heed? Preach My presence, please. I beg you, be alone with Me, experience My heartache, My pain to be ignored and suffer such indifference! I am allowing you to be united to Me in such a way that you will suffer some of My feelings. Oh, sweet one, I want your all. You hold on to this life. Such details, such sufferings people endure for such useless things!

Surrender your all to Me. When the road is hard and you think, "Oh, Jesus, what do You want from me?," focus on Me, right by your side, instructing you and telling you to quit fighting your crosses. Accept your crosses and grow in your love of Me. I give you little gems in your crosses. No one ever knows what I am teaching you. I teach you exactly as you need. Accept the cross and be taught by the Son of God.

Your weariness and tiredness is telling you that you need to be at home. Do not go running around. Stay fixed to your children and play with them. Your time with others is displeasing to Me. You have time, but when you get to your children, you are worn out. You are not being with them. Surrender to My wishes. I want you with your children tomorrow. If others call you, tell them you have to be with your children. Talk to others about Me and never talk to your children. Your job is to teach them about My ardent love. You are not doing My Will when you shove them back and talk to others. They are more important to your work for Me than you will ever know. They need your talking and being with them. It displeases

Me when you ignore your promptings and give in to others. Please harken to My call to be close to your children.

April 8, 1994
I Come Into Your Heart

R. How can I be focused on myself when the Son of God is within my breast? This is His aching when I receive God, Who has come to me in such love, and then I focus on all my incidental problems. He wants our love, our longing, our joy to behold the Son of God in our hearts and we focus on such incidentals and worries!

Oh, how could you do this to Me when the Son of God enters your breast and comes into your heart and you ignore Me or worry for such nonsense? Be with Me, be in love with Me. Let yourself go of the cares of the world and focus on Me alone, out of such love to come and dwell in your breast.

I am the Son of God and I am in your breast this very day because I love you. How it wounds Me when you ignore Me and look the other way and focus on your incidental worldly cares. Oh, be with Me, please. I come with such love. God enters your breast and I am with you, inside of your heart. Put away all the cares of this world and just be with your Lover.

I am the Sacred Heart of Jesus and I love you so much, My child.

April 10, 1994
Do My Will

You must not get discouraged. I need you to do this work. They persecuted Me, they mocked Me, they tore My flesh, and what had I done?

You must obey Me, even if you do not want to. It is every command I give you that is to be obeyed. If others prevent you from obeying My Will, it is their fault. I want every letter of every law obeyed in these letters. Do not ever underestimate the order of obedience. You must do My Will. Listen to your heart and obey Me always!

You cannot ever ignore My wishes. Your heart will gnaw at you until you obey. Take care of yourself and obey My Will. You must always obey Me to the letter of the law!

You are dealing with the Son of God. You are being told what to do by God. If you do not obey Me, you do not feel good. You obey as I command you. Always obey your superiors.

I am Jesus, the Son of God. This is not a myth. I am truly speaking to you. I will protect you, child. Surrender to Me. All I allow to happen is for you to learn a lesson. You must realize the very hairs of your head are numbered. Accept all your discomforts and learn the lessons I so sweetly teach. Suffering I allow. Accept everything as coming from Him Who ardently loves you!

I am Jesus, the Son of God, and I am speaking to you, child. Hear Me and be taught by Him Who ardently loves you. I am all powerful. I want you to do this work. If the whole world does not believe, it is not your problem. Detach from people and do your job. Tend to your family first. Do not be busy pleasing others. Give them many letters. They can learn from them. You are the messenger. You have a family. You only write and speak to groups.

I will tend to My letters. You do not have to prove anything to anyone. If they are curious about you, do not answer. Only preach the messages. You receive letters for them from Me. You are the receiver. If they want to listen, they will be wise and hear My love for them. If they do not, they will miss a great gift I am giving freely to them.

You are not responsible for giving anyone your precious time to convince them these are for real. You are responsible for your children, for praying and playing with them. Tell others your demands are great to spend much time in prayer and to be with your children. I am very displeased with the time you do not spend with your family.

When you decide you will do good works, but do not do what I am telling you to do, you are doing your own will. You are not feeling good. How do I get your attention? I can stop you. Then you will listen. I want you to obey Me always. I am God and I am speaking here. My Will is as you are prompted in your heart. If you do not obey Me, you are doing what you want.

You fret, you fume, you worry, you want to please others. You are too connected to others and to making yourself valid. You have valid letters from Jesus Christ. If they need to check you out, it is their problem. You have jobs to do for Me. Pray and be with Me, with your children. I want you to speak. I will take care of you, child. When will you surrender? Let go and totally trust in Me. You are a human. You are not perfect. If others want you so, just forget their demands. They are not perfect. They have no right to demand you to act a certain way for their liking. People should be busy about themselves and how holy they are. To see how holy their brother is is not their affair at all.

If you are without fault, then you can cast the first stone. Be not attached to your brother and how he is acting. Do not judge and make yourself right and them wrong. This is from Satan. No one has power over you but Me. Surrender yourself, body and soul, to Me. Do as I tell you. Pray with your children and take them to Mass. Your job is to trust Me totally, to surrender to Me, to do My Will as I dictate in your heart. You have no time for visiting or for idle talk.

You are a messenger. You are not to be analyzed and checked out. Whatever people do, that is their problem, not yours. If they need to do that, they miss time learning what I am teaching you.

I am Jesus Christ, the Son of God. I write and talk to you. You know the things I tell you. You experience the emotions I let you feel. If others listen, they will share in My relationship with you. If they do not, they miss great treasures I am imparting to you. Satan is busy blocking the message. The message is coming from God. He will do all he can to stop My words to My beloved ones. Listen and be taught. Your time is very precious to Me. I want it spent with Me and with your children. You have no time for idle chitchat. Your job is very demanding.

I will care to every detail in your life. If the whole world misses the message, it is not your concern. You are the receiver. If I ask you to speak to a group, I will speak directly through you. Your only job is to pray first. I am using your voice to give messages. Keep singing the songs I tell you to sing. If I want to touch one person, you obey Me. Whatever I tell you to do, you do it, if you like it or not. This pleases Me greatly.

I love you so, child. I love you. You are faithfully serving Me. You are being taught. Do not be prideful for being admonished, but be open to Him Who loves you to His death, Him Who loves you more than you love yourself. All I give and tell you is from My great love for you. Be open, surrender, and be about My work. Time is so short! I cannot tell you how it will all go up in your face. You will let go then. I need you to let go now and do My Will.

R. I am being taught every day. I must learn to surrender and realize He has all the power and accept my trials. I want to serve only Him. I live only for love of Him and love of my brothers. As soon as I become anxious, Satan has stepped in with his bag of tricks. Satan is a great deceiver. He talks in my head to stop God's work. I love Jesus so! I must operate only for love of Him and my brothers. I must do God's Will!

Focus Only on My Love

Come to Me, all who are weary and heavily burdened, and I will give you rest. I have not come to give you glory in this world. I have come to save you from your sins. I have come, for such love I have for you.

You will be persecuted beyond belief, mostly by priests. Do not give in to any persecution. You can withstand all that you are given. You focus only on My love. Your life is lived only to spread the love of Jesus. Your brothers in darkness will hate you. Hate and anger are always from Satan. I am Peace. I am Love. I come to save and show sinners the way to love.

A heart given to Jesus is a tender heart. It is not ever given to hate and anger. It is full of love. A heart of Jesus responds with love when attacked. A heart of Jesus detaches itself from the self and only responds with love. You know how deeply I love you. You know a little of My love. You do not have any idea of My love. If you ever knew of My immense love, you would never be afraid of anything. You would be at total peace.

Focus on the immensity of My love, child. I truly loved you to My death. Think how you feel when you are loved by a human. It is a feeling of peace and joy to know love. This is mere mortals giving imperfect love and you are given to such peace. I am God. I am Jesus Christ. I am Love. I am so full of love for you, perfect love, not the imperfect love of humans, but immense, longing, on-fire ardent love, love that never flickers, love that loves you in your darkest hour! Your whole answer to persecution is to know that you function only for love of Me and the immense burning love I have for you. I am God. I have all the power and I love you this way. Focus on being this loved. This sets you free. Your peace comes from these two facts.

Oh, how I love you, little ones! Think about Me, hanging there in such horrid agony, and in My mind are only thoughts of love for you. I am Jesus Christ. I am the living God. I am in your midst and I am loving you this way, this very day. You do not fret. You do not fear. You focus on My love coming—so immense you cannot comprehend—and it comes to you at every second. It never stops.

Suffer your persecution. When they persecute you for My sake, great is your reward in heaven. When they persecute you, they persecute Me. I suffer for the loss of love of My blessed priests. Pray for My priests. Pray constantly. Offer sacrifices for those souls who are hurting. You have no time to ever listen to anyone's persecution.

I need this work accomplished. People need to know of My ardent, on-fire, gentle love.

You remain always loving. Do not ever respond with anger and hate, respond with the gentleness of love. I give you My strength. I give you My love. You can love others because I have loved you first.

Oh, what do I say to convince you? I died for you with such love, and you ask for more! I give Myself to you, Body and Blood, Soul and Divinity, in the Eucharist. I remain forever in the tabernacle with such ardent love!

Oh, child, do not listen to those who attack you. I need you to speak of My love. I give you all you need. Pray constantly for your attackers. I love them so. Your love will preach My lessons.

Never lose your peace. Love God, love one another. Eye has not seen, ear has not heard the glory that awaits him who loves and serves the Lord! I am Jesus. I am the Living God. I am with you, little one. Believe Me. Do not believe a sick world. My love will see you through.

Think of Me, loving you. Focus on it. I am God and I gave My life for you because I loved you so. You are so precious to Me. You are My beautiful child. I love you so much. You will never know how much I love you. I wait for you to come and be in union with Me. Let go of your world. Nothing here can compare to the love of God.

My babies, I love you. Read this letter when your heart is troubled. Do not be troubled. You will know such peace when you focus on My love. Love God, love one another. It is so simple! Man has made it so complicated! Let go of yourselves and live. Live in My love! I am Jesus and I am in your midst this very day. I love you so. I love you. Jesus.

April 11, 1994

You Are the Light

Where is the light I give to you, My daughter? Your light is dimmed by the words of Satan to stop you. I am God and I am speaking to you. These letters are for My beloved ones. I have chosen to write to you, for them. You must hold tightly to your call to be the light shining in the darkest night.

I am the Alpha and the Omega. This is no myth, My child. Get a hold on Satan and cast him into the fires of hell. My work needs to be done. You will lead many to My Sacred Heart. I love you so intently, yet you do not hear. You listen to the idle words of those who are sick and Satan plays them in your head!

Your Last Chance to Love

The way to Me is the way of the cross. You will wear My crown but it will not be a crown of glory, but a crown of thorns. You, My child, are loved so dearly by Me. Suffer with Me, but never doubt anything I tell you. I am God and I am speaking to you. What must I do to convince you? You doubt because Satan wants this stopped. Do not give in to him.

My child, My child, My favored, blessed child, I give you crosses because I love you. You I have loved dearly all through your life. Your crosses have brought you to Me and My love. Life will soon be over on this earth for you. All that matters are the things of God. Love all those around you as if it be your last chance to love. Live each day to love all around you. Live it as if it be your last day to live on this earth. Would you waste valuable time fuming and fretting? Time is short and souls will be lost. They will suffer the loss of their souls. You do not have time for any remorse. Your job is to preach My ardent love to My beloved ones. There is so much sin and so much blindness, but the kingdom of God awaits all those who love and serve the Lord.

Please, I beg of you, spread My love. Do not let Satan get you focused on yourself. Your work is to lead souls to My most ardent love. What an honor! I am awaiting My precious ones. Have faith, child. I am truly writing to you and I am God. I gave My all for love of you, My child. I died that you might live. Give yourself to Me now.

Anger Is Destructive—Love Heals

R. Love is healing. If you attack me and I respond with love by the grace of God, but let it fester later into anger, I have an active emotion inside of me. You hurt me. I was right, you were wrong. I get angry or I get depressed. Some action occurs within me. If, by the grace of God, I acted lovingly when you attacked me, then, when I go away, I must continue to dismiss any thoughts of how I have been wronged and beg God for His help to forgive and love you.

April 12, 1994 After Communion at St. Gertrude Church
Satan's Way Is Division

To preach the gospel in your very being, you must always be fixed in My love. When they tore My flesh, I loved them. I at no time responded to them with anything but love. The way to Me is the way of love. I forgave them. I forgive you for your sins.

You must always love and forgive. When they persecute you and holler every slander against you, remember the way to Me is love. Love those who persecute you. Love your attackers. Love your brothers. Love is action from the hearts. It is not lip service. Love is giving. Love is action. Love mends broken fences.

Satan's way is division, hatred, anger. These create such a destructive force! It is an energy that tears at the hearts of men. It is transmitted and lives in hearts, just as My love is transmitted and lives in hearts.

Purify your heart at every second. Keep it so clean. Do not let any anger, resentment, hatred for your brothers mount up by the side of your heart. Flush it away. Pray, pray, pray for grace. Pray for love. Pray for your brothers. You need My love to respond with love. I give you freely of My love when you ask. I am the source of all love. You come, you partake, you give to your brothers as I have given to you. Love is a force. It is a mighty life. It is a light that shines brightest in the darkest night.

Be at peace. Be full of joy. I am God. Do not fret or fume or doubt. Do not be angry or feel you have been wronged. These are from the evil one.

I am in control. I am God. I am by your side this very day in that cross you carry. You in your pain will learn My mighty lessons of love. I am molding you and shaping you into My mighty soldiers, soldiers in My army of love!

Be open, pray for love, pray for the grace to forgive. See Me dying on the cross. I held not back. I gave the last drop of My blood, the last beat of My Heart, for love of you! Can you not forgive your hurting brothers? I need you to love those who hurt you. I need you to forgive those who injure you. You are My soldiers. You will fight My battle for My loved ones. You will carry the flag of love to those who are hurting.

Forgive all those who hurt you and pray for them. Love is the answer. My way is the way of love. Love finds the way to peace. If you want peace, you must forgive and let go. You must trust totally in Me and know that I will never desert you. My hand is in everything you experience. I allow suffering for a reason. You learn mighty lessons in your trials. You are purified in your sufferings. You can gain many graces for yourselves and others when you accept all I give you with love. I give you love. I give you what you need. Let go and surrender to Me, My little, beloved ones. I never ever leave your side!

April 13, 1994

I Give You All You Need

I am the Good Shepherd. I know Mine and they follow Me. Come, My little lambs, follow My ways. I am truly your Savior. When you are hungry, I give you to eat. When you need for anything, I know your needs. I ponder the way of your heart. Surrender your lives to Me, little, scared ones. Have no fear. I am God and I give you all you need. I am God. I am mighty. Why do you fear when I, God, watch out for you?

You wander, you wane in and out, and I am truly here. You get full of self, you think you need to find a way for yourself. You need to remain rooted in love and give of yourself. I will care for your needs. You do not have to fight a beaten path for what is important. I yield to you exactly what you need in all My gentleness and love! You only need to stay fixed in Me and trust in Me for all things. Anger is a force that tells you you need to take control. You need to have your way. I tell you to remain selfless, to surrender, to let go. Holding on is draining. "I will keep track of this little thing I have with you and that thing with you." Such a waste of your energy and your valuable time when I could have loved! You choose selfishness, caring for yourself. When does it end? Do you get enough to feed the starved self? Only the love of God feeds your hungry soul!

Only love of God, love of your neighbor, gives you peace. Do you want peace or power? Do you ever have enough power? Do you want to promote yourself or be free? You are already so very special. You were created by God and you are so perfect, so beautiful, so precious. You are the only soul like you and I love you dearly as you are. You are My prized loved one. Oh, how I love you! You are the perfect creation of My Father, My little, beloved one. I love you so. The Father loves you, the Holy Spirit loves you, the Blessed Mother loves you. You are My precious one. You are perfect and I love you as you are. I loved you to My death.

Do not let your heart be busy feeling bowed down and anxious. Come to Me and be filled by My ardent love. I love you intensely at this moment. I am Jesus, the Son of God. You are My beloved ones. To My death I loved each one of you. Do not be angered at your brother. Love him as I love you. Light up the darkness with the love of God in your heart.

I am Jesus and I love you.

(Letter for Front of B.B. II)
April 13, 1994

I Love You

How, child, do I, Jesus, tell you I love you? You hold on to silly things, when God is in your midst and is ardently loving you. I am Jesus Christ, the Son of God. I am writing to each precious child this day. I am on fire for love of you. I remain in the Eucharist to be with you with My ardent love. I did not want to leave My beloved ones at the Last Supper. I love you so, My dear and ardently loved children. I remain with you this day in the Blessed Sacrament, the same Jesus Who died a brutal death on the cross.

Do you know I am truly present there? Do you know that God waits every day for you in the tabernacle? Do you comprehend even a minute amount of My love? You will never on earth know how I love you.

I, Jesus, truly the Son of God, came to earth a man and suffered a brutal death for love of you. I love you so much! I remain with you this day. I long for your love. I want you to come and be with Me in front of the tabernacle. I wait, I yearn for you to come and whisper your love to Me. I am a Person and I love you this day with such an ardent, on-fire love. No human could ever compare a speck to My love for you.

I wait, little ones, in the tabernacle. I wait for you to come and receive Me in Communion. I want you to want Me so much that you cannot wait to come and receive Me. I want to be the love, the Center of your life!

I am Jesus. I am the Son of God. I am writing to you this day. I want to possess your very soul and live in you. I have all you need, sweet ones. Oh, you are so blind! I long for your union with Me. I wrote the book on love. I instituted it, yet you go to the world for your love and do not even come to Me! Oh, I love you, little ones. Little ones, beloved of the Father, loved by the Holy Spirit, mothered by My very own mother, what more can I say? The rest is up to you!

I give you your will with such love and I want your love, freely given. I am God. What do you think you could ever need that I do not give you? I am the Savior of this world. I am Jesus, the Son of God. I am waiting for you. I am longing for you. I am yearning for you. I am God. I have all you ever will need!

Surrender this life to Me. Pray My prayer for union with Me. I want to possess your soul and operate from your very being. I am Jesus. I am the Son of God. I am the Sacred Heart of Jesus. I am Who am. I died and rose on the third day.

Harken to My call, harken to My pleading. Spend your days in love with Me. Nothing matters unless it is rooted in Me and rooted in My love. I am the Son of God. I am the Sacred Heart of Jesus. I love you with the tenderest love. I am waiting this day for you, My beloved one. Come to Me for I am the tenderest of all hearts. I am the Sacred Heart of Jesus.

April 13, 1994 at St. Gertrude Church   3:30p.m.
He Mounts His Throne

R. The King of Glory is on His throne. He is so beautiful! His throne is not a throne adorned in jewels, but a brown, wooden cross. He has on His throne the look of total surrender. He gave His all in ardent love. He had not the superior look as that of a king, but the humble, surrendering look of our beloved Jesus, God. He is our King. He asks us for our love. Do we look to the kings of the world and mount our throne adorned in glory, full of self, or do we mount a throne He has prepared for us, one full of selflessness and suffering? The way to this King is but one way—it is the way of the cross. Through His cross and resurrection we are saved. He won for us the battle over our sins and paid the price of salvation with His blood.

Do I mount the throne He has prepared for me? Do I wear the crown of thorns or the crown of glory in this life? Only by our surrender are we made His heirs. It is only in our modeling after Him that we receive the reward promised. It is eternal salvation into His kingdom! Do I wear His crown or look for a useless crown of worldly glory?

The way to You is the way of the cross, to take up this cross and follow in Your footsteps. Will I follow? Will I wander and lay my cross down?

Oh, it feels good to take care of yourself, to tend to every hair and every piece of clothing, to eat the finest food and go to the theater. Oh, it feels good for a moment, only to need the next moment's gratification.

Oh, the soul craves the love of God. The soul thirsts after the love of God. Do I attempt to feed my soul with the things of this world, only to find that I soon need another feeding, and another, and another. Yet I am never satisfied. I hunger and thirst more.

Oh, what feeds the starving soul? Only He Who took up His cross and showed us the way. The way to Him is the only way. He showed us by His very life. He, God, came to this earth a mere human and gave to us His very life that we might live. He walked the steps of this earth so we could model ourselves after Him. What love, to give His very life for us!

Little ones, preach My ardent love. Do not let a day go by that you do not tell someone how I am Jesus and I am in your midst this very day. Tell them how I long for them and wait for them and want to be with them so.

I am full of love. I have all they need. They come empty, they leave full. My abundance I pour out to them. Do you expect any the less from Him Who died for you! Oh, little, precious ones, I want to give you My love. Share My love with your brothers. I am the Sacred Heart of Jesus. I am on fire. I never grow cold. I never grow tired of loving you. Come and let Me minister to your sorrowing hearts. I am Whom you seek. I am here waiting for you. Feed your souls, children. They are thirsting for the love of God. I have all you need.

I am Jesus, the Son of God. I love you. Amen.

April 14, 1994 After Communion
Be with Me in Communion

My tenderness, My love, My goodness, My presence I pour out to you in the Eucharist. You run from My altar to be about your busyness. I am God. I yearn and long for you so! Oh, if you only knew how I want you to sit and wait with Me. I cry for your love. I ache so in My Heart to give you My ardent love.

You receive Me, you leave, and I write in these letters to you, My beloved ones. What more can I tell you? I want you to know Me intimately. I am truly present in the Eucharist you receive. It wounds Me so to watch you run from Me, when I, God, want so much for you to stay and be with Me.

Oh, little ones, I love you, I love you, I love you. I am sorrowful for your neglect and indifference. This is so painful to My aching Heart, to be neglected and treated so indifferently. I am so tender in My love for you. Sit with Me. Do not be busy for such useless tasks. I am suffering from your indifference. I love you this day.

Let Go!

R. Why should I get anxious about anything? All that matters is that
I do what He wants me to do. He wants me to love Him and love
my brothers.

How is the tone of your voice? Is it gentle? How do you talk to
your children and your special loved ones? Are you less loving to
your family? Always calmness, always love. No need to fret or
fume. Where are you going? What do you have to do? Do you yell
anxiously at your family and demand their attention, by your tone?
Do you demand urgency by a summoning tone or do you display a
tone of peace and love when you talk to all?

If I am tending to your every need, why do you have to get so
irritated? Are you tending to your needs and being irritated because
it isn't done to your liking?

I call you to peace. Let go of your irritations. Do not get angered.
Accept things as they are. Each person has a right to be. Why do
you have a right to tell them how to be? Mind your own affairs. You
have lots to learn to be kind and gentle and loving. You are going
nowhere. You do not even know how irritable you are. Listen to
yourself, demanding your way, snapping at your beloved ones. Oh,
but you have to get the job done! Right. For what reason? Be at
peace. I tend to the lilies of the fields and the birds of the air. I tend
to the babies in the womb. Do you hear anyone yelling to get the
job done?

I am peace. I am assuredness. My ways are truth and right. My
ways are calm and direct. I do not yell or tell you to get the job
done for Me. I let you be and you make mistakes, but I let you have
your free will. You have a free will. If you choose to make your will
the Will of God, everything works in such harmony. You do not
need to demand your way. You do not have to shout urgent pleas to
your brothers.

Let go, let yourself go. Feel the freedom of surrender. You tug up
the hill, you puff, you pant. I come to you and give you a powerful
push. All of a sudden you operate with no effort. This is life with
Me, when you surrender. You pray hard, you push hard, you yell
hard, you *are* hard! Let go of yourself. My way is easy. You are
going nowhere too late or too soon. You are operating in My world.
Your only job is to love Me and love each other. When you push to
make someone move as you want, you are in control. You do not
need force if I am in control.

I make things happen. I know exactly what is going on in the air, the ground, your hearts, your heads, your bodies. I know all things. When will you surrender and come to Me for your answers? Silly ones! I am God. I loved you to My death. Do you not think I would care for you this day if I died for you? I love you. I give you what you need. Cling to Me. Be attentive to Me. Surrender yourself. Come and pray to Jesus in the tabernacle and after Communion. What wisdom!

I am God. Where I am, Father and Holy Spirit are present. Oh, I love you. Mary is your loving mother. Surrender, little ones. Do not run your lives. Pray My Prayer for Union with Me.

Your lives will truly change. I am the Alpha. I am the Omega. I am God. Do not yell at the lilies! What a useless task! Do you think you will make them grow prettier or faster? Let go, be at peace, surrender to Him Who ardently loves you. Oh, little ones, let your hearts pant for love of Me. I love you so. Feel a flutter in your chest at the mention of My name.

I am truly here this day, waiting to release you from your anxieties. I am Jesus, the Son of God. I am your beautiful Shepherd. I know mine and they follow Me. Surrender, little, beloved ones. I want to caress you and lead you down My path. I am the Good Shepherd. I am Who am. I am here this day. Come to Me in communion and sit for long periods. These are the golden moments, in communion. Oh, sweet ones, know Me, love Me, serve Me. I am God and I love you so!

April 14, 1994
He Communicates in Our Hearts and Souls

R. What do You look like, Jesus? Does it matter what You look like? What matters is how we are in our hearts. We know You, Jesus. We love You in our hearts. It doesn't matter, Jesus, what I look like or what I wear. All that matters is how I am kind and loving. When will we learn that what matter are the things of the soul, what we are in our hearts. Oh, Jesus, teach me to let go of the world and my attachments to things that do not matter. Help me to see with the eyes of God. You do not look at our hair, our bodies, or our clothes. You look to our souls. You ponder our hearts. You love us just as we are. So why do I worry about such things? Teach me to know, with the heart of God, all I need to know about my brothers. He does not care of their education. He cares for *them*. Teach me to love with the Heart of God. He loves us unconditionally.

He loves us, His little, dear children. Despite how we act, He loves us as we are. Teach me to love You, Jesus, to know You, Jesus, and to serve You, Jesus, so I can see as You see me, Jesus, not as I see myself.

Jesus, when You look at my brothers, You see *them*. You do not see their gray hair, their blonde hair, or their black hair. You see *them*. You do not see their size and shape. You see *them*. Teach me, Jesus, to see my brothers as You see them, not to size them up, see their exterior, and judge them by that. Oh, Jesus, teach me to see and feel with the eyes and heart of God so I can love my brothers as You do.

Puff and Toot

R. My daughter played the song *Puff and Toot* and we sang and laughed. "I've got to make it! I've got to make it! I've got to make it!" Sometimes when I do it myself, I try so hard. I try so hard to do everything right. Think of going up a big hill and huffing and puffing. Then the hand of God reaches down and lifts you. He carries you on your way.

This is how it has been in my life. When I pray over people, I would lay my hands down very hard. When I pray over people and barely touch them, I can feel a strong power take over. When I sang, I would try so hard to sound good. Jesus told me to sing gently. When I let go, He sings through me. With every thing, when I am trying so hard, I am doing it. When He does it, I feel a power carrying it out.

How Did I Treat You Today?

R. How did I treat you this day, you, very special soul, created by God? You are God's precious child. Were you treated harshly when you were little, or has someone wronged you this very day, or are you sick and suffering? I do not know all the details of your life, but I do know you are a precious child of God and you are my brother.

How did I treat you this day? Did I think how much God loves you and wants you with Him forever in heaven? Did I think about your soul when I saw you hurting? I want to go to heaven and I want to be there with you. You are my brother and I love you.

I knew you were hurting today and I didn't see your soul. I only listened to your angry words and tolerated you and walked away. I made myself right and thought about you with anger. I told others and felt more right and knew you were definitely wrong. I didn't feel good inside. I knew you were suffering. Could I not have smiled and forgotten your anger and prayed for your aching heart? I know you are my brother. I want to be in heaven with you. You needed God's love today. Did I love you for Him or did I walk away?

I want to love like you. The more I know what You are asking me to do, the more I know how truly beautiful a Person You are. Jesus, it is hard to love our brothers when they wrong us. Jesus, it is hard to forgive their misdeeds. Jesus, You forgave those who tore Your flesh. The way to You, Lord, is love and forgiveness!

My child, you do not do anything alone. When you come to Me in the Eucharist and in front of the tabernacle, I give you special graces to help you love. I shower you with My love. I fill you with such gifts you cannot receive anywhere on the face of this earth.

Do you, My beloved ones, want to love your brothers? Do you want to know My ways and live in harmony with Me? Come to Me in My Blessed Sacrament and let Me minister to you. The time you spend after Communion is your dearest treasure. Do not run from My altar to get to your world. Stay and let Me bathe you in My beautiful love! I bathe you. You leave with such beautiful love to share with your beloved ones.

I call you to give My love to My hurting brothers. I call you to love them for Me. I call you to minister love to them.

R. How did I treat you this day? Did I treat you with His love? Do I really want to touch you so you will go to heaven? Did I miss a golden opportunity to share God's love with you when you needed it so badly?

How did I preach the gospel to you this day? Do I really love you, my brother?

Go to Confession

I am the Way, the Truth, and the Life. I am your Jesus of Mercy. I forgive every sin if you come to Me in Confession. The priest is My representative. You need the sacrament of confession. You need to come and lay your faults before Me. My mercy is so abundant! I give so freely to you who are sorry for your sins.

Please come to Me. Please come and sit with Me and ask Me for guidance to teach you My love. I will show you My way. My way is to love Me above all things and to love one another. Will you love

Me? Will you love your brothers? The way to Me is love. Come to Me in Communion and in front of the tabernacle and I will shower you with My love.

May You Live in Me and I in You

R.I know You, God, in my heart. When I focus on Your being in me and my life in You, when I pray the Prayer for Union with You, when I surrender more and more of me and give myself to You, we are so closely united. I want to be one in You and You in me. This oneness is that which speaks in my heart. The more I am connected with You, the more my heart knows You, knows Your ways, loves from You, loves my brothers from You. I seek this oneness with You, Lord. Anything I am attached to keeps me from union with You. Anything I make my god keeps me from making You number one.

Oh, Lord, treat me gently and help me to surrender to You. I want to live, me in You and You in me. Teach me Your ways. I love You so. Where am I going in my huff and puff? You are what matters most to me. I love You.

Rita

Strip Yourself of Worldly Pleasures

What rewards await you! Blessed are they who have not seen and have believed. You do not need to see Me with your eyes. You need to know Me in your heart. Do you want to have union with Me? Deny yourself. You can only feel Me in your heart. Open it wide, clean it out, spray it with My grace and love, pray, go to Confession, receive the Blessed Sacrament. Be about the job at hand. My work is found in having an intimate union with Me. We become as one—I communicate in you and you know Me in your head. So you know when I want you to do something? Yes, you do. You feel it very strongly in your heart and it nags at you until you do it. I do not let you go. I want you to listen to My promptings.

Oh, do I love you! Die to yourself, child. You are so attached. I am He Who loves and sustains you. I am God. Let go and I will take care of your every need. I am Jesus, Son of God. Cling to Me and let Me operate inside of you. You are My beloved one.

Is Your Glass Half-Full or Half-Empty?

R. How is your day? Is your glass half-full or half-empty? This is the gauge to how you are feeling inside. Are you seeing all the blessings He is pouring out to you—your health, your food, your loved ones, all the blessings that you have each day? Or are you coming from a place of never having enough? Do you feel irritable and feel that nothing is right, that everything is wrong?

Is the glass half-full or is it half-empty? Do you look for things that are right in your world or do you look for things that are wrong? Do you know that God gives to you exactly what you need and that it is in your acceptance of these things that you grow in your relationship with Him?

Is the glass half-full or half-empty? Do I look at the world and see the love of God in my brothers? Do I look at the world and see the world as not giving to me?

God has all you need. God provides us with our needs. The world is hurting. The world is not that by which we are filled. The world cries from its own pain. How can the world fill us?

We crave the love of God. Our souls can only be satisfied by the love of God. When we see the world as a place that needs God's love, we come to the world with a full glass.

How is your glass today? Is it half-full or half-empty? If you go to our beloved Jesus, He fills you with His love. His love is emitted from your very being. When you spend time with Him and remain fixed in Him, there is peace in His love.

The biggest contribution you can give to yourself and this world is to busy yourself with your relationship with Jesus. Be an empty vessel (glass) ready to be filled by His love.

I Guard Your Way

Come to Me and I give you rest. When you were hungry, I gave you to eat. When you were naked, I clothed you. You are the salt of the earth. You are the city on a hill shining into this dark world. Let the light of God's love shine from your very soul.

Do not fret or fume or feel anxious for I am God and I am guarding your way. I do not talk to you and then forget you. I care for you as I care for the lilies of the field. You are so precious to Me. All those who go with you are guarded by the hand of God. You are the city. You are set on the hill. Your light shines brightest in the darkest night. Satan wants to stop you. Cast him out and pray for My grace. I am God. You do not worry for I, God, watch you by day and guard you at night. My hand is upon you. My love is forever with you.

In adversity, do not fume, do not fret. Hold tight, for God protects you on your way. You will receive this grace from Me in abundance and I will go with you to guard you.

Do you think I would send you there to have you suffer? I send you there to be renewed. Do not worry, child. My hand is forever with you.

I am the Son of God. I have all the power. Your peace in all trials will teach you My might. I am the Almighty God. I am Jesus Christ, your shield, your refuge. I am your beloved and I am God. You know Him Who is in high places. Cling to Me and be attentive to Me now and forever. I love you. Amen.

Be not troubled, sweet one, I am your Savior. I allow with love all that happens to you. I do not hand you a snake. I only give according to your needs. I am your Jesus, your Beloved One. Do not be anxious for anything. Do not fret or fume. I am the same Jesus Who died for love of you, and would die for you this very day. I am the Savior of this world. I go with you wherever you go. I come and you are set free. Freedom is complete trust in Me. Do you trust Me or do you think you trust Me? Let go and put your life and that of your beloved ones in the hands of Jesus Christ.

See Me, My child, bloodied, bruised and beaten for love of you. Do you think I would come to earth with such love for you and then not guard you? I guard you as a treasure. I treasure you and your life. Your life will be with Me in heaven. Do not worry for I am God and I am guarding you, this very day. Love Me, keep My commandments, love one another.. that is all I ask.

R.Love is from God. Love is only as it draws others to God. If my love for you does not draw you closer to God, then it is not love.

Love is for you, My beloved. I give it freely. Love Me and love one another. Do not fret, I am here. In all adversity, remain fixed in My love and trust in My ways. I am ever by your side. I never slumber or sleep. I guard you, My beloved ones, I guard you.

Trust Me. A mighty lesson in trust you will receive. Let go and do not focus on anything but My love for you. I go by your side. The very hairs of your head are numbered. Sit tight constantly and pray to Him Who has all the power. I will be with you wherever you go. Do not ever lose your peace for I sustain you. This will strengthen your trust in Me. Tell your children to trust in Me and My ways. There is nothing to fear for I go with you. My hand is in everything you experience. Accept all things as coming from Him Who loves you dearly and grow in your relationship with Me.

I am God. Be calm. Do not be rattled by anything. I am there in your midst and I guard you, My beloved ones. I guard you personally.

April 19, 1994 at Father Smith's Chapel   **9:45a.m.**

How Do I Love Thee, Jesus?

R. How do I love You, Jesus? I love You according to where I am in my heart. Do I judge my brothers—some are okay and some I want to avoid? Do I see with Your eyes, God, every child most precious to You.

How do I love You, Jesus? Am I eager to spread Your love to the hurting ones as well as the nice ones? Do I remember how You loved all to Your death? You did not die just for some. You died for the precious love of each and every soul.

How do I love You, Jesus? Do I love You in my brothers this day, or do I think, "Tomorrow I will love them all the way He wants." Every minute of every day is an opportunity for me to love my hurting brothers. If I miss moments in this day to love, they miss the love You want to give to them through me.

How do I love You, Jesus? How will I love the people You put in my path today? Will I love at all? Will my heart be fixed on You, or will I think of my own selfish interests and let a golden opportunity slip through my fingers?

How did I love You, Jesus, this day? I cannot love, Jesus, as You did. I need Your Heart to live in me. I need my heart to be filled with Your love. Oh, Jesus, let me join my heart to Yours. Teach me to love, as You so desire, all my brothers with a heart of love.

How did I love You, Jesus, this day? I need You, Lord. I need Your grace. I need You joined to me. Make me selfless and empty, ready to be filled by You. Help me to love with a heart full of Your love. Your way is not easy, Lord. I cannot do it without You, working in me. Join my heart in love to You that I might love as You desire. I love You, Jesus, my Lord, my God, my all. How can I love You as I ought? Do I want to love You, Lord, in my brothers? Do I choose to love?

Do I forgive, Lord? Do I forgive as You did when You forgave those who crucified You? Do I see how You showed me the way to love? You are so beautiful, Lord. You showed the way to love and forgiveness. Teach me Your ways, Lord. When You taught them Your ways of love, Lord, You were not popular. They persecuted You. They did not want to hear Your ways. Help me to be open, Lord, to the changes You want to occur in me so I can grow to be the light You want to shine in this dark world.

My child, there is no growth if the plant remains the same. Be ready to be pruned and plucked, cut back, watered, fertilized. Growth is not always easy, but what a beautiful plant in the end. Be ready for the pruning. Be ready for all that I send you. Be open and ready, for the day of the Lord is at hand. Every day you will be used to help others to grow in My love. Your trials are necessary for your growth. Without the trials you will not learn the teachings you need to do the work. Be an open door, accept all I send through the door and praise Him Who loves you dearly.

You are the light of the world. A city set on a hill will shine brightly with the love of God radiating from the hearts of those who dwell there. I call you, My child, to love one another. This will light the darkest night. I am your Jesus, Son of the Living God. I am that light that shines from you. Be open to Me. Be ready, for My day is at hand and I operate from you. I love you, My beloved ones. Harken to My call. It is an urgent call from Him Who loves you dearly and cries out for the love of My beloved little ones who are in darkness. Do not be distracted by this world. Focus on Me and My love. I am the light that shines in the darkness. Let My light shine from your souls.

April 22, 1994
Listen of My Intense Love

On a bus.

You must find time to be alone with Me. Take time and focus on Me all through the day. I wanted you on this trip. Pray constantly. Do not waste one moment. I am your God and I love you. Do not waste precious time. Always spread My love to My beloved ones. I love you.

At Father Joza's Church

My dear child, write to Me. You must write when I call you to write. Put yourself into a smoke screen. We are alone. Feel My presence. Forget the world and let go totally to Me. Do not focus on anyone but Me. See My suffering face. See Me, My child, and know of My love for each person. I am so ardently in love with each and every one. When you focus on My crucifixion you will become closer and closer to Me. See My face, dying on the cross. I am the Son of God. You are My beloved one.

Think only of Me. Block out all those around you and be with Me. This is a place to pray to Me. Any distractions are not your problem. Be alone, be with Me, entirely alone and in union with Me. Block out all that is around you. You can write on a plane—anywhere. You must harken to Me when I call you. Listen to My intense love for you. Be alone with Me now. I love you.

You Are My Vessel to Reach Many

My dear child, I want you to spread My love. This is My work for you. You are My messenger. If you do not speak, no one will hear. I love each child so uniquely and you must tell all how much I wait and want to be with them. If you do not speak, no one will hear.

Come to Me, My precious one, beloved of My Father. You are so loved! Your glory will come in the world to come. Tend only to the job at hand. Your job is to spread My love. Tell every person you can how I am waiting to be with them. Give them a Prayer for Union with Me. Pray for them. Any person I send to you is one you need to speak to. Speak to them. A few words on My love will make a big difference in their life. People are suffering. They are waiting to find that which I and I alone can give them. They long for My love. Oh, little one, feed their hungry souls with My letters. Never miss an opportunity to spread My letters or My love. I am counting on you. Your job is to be My messenger. Please, I beg of you, you must spread this work for Me! Time, My child, is so short. Souls are at stake. I have given you personal love letters from Me.

Do not fume, do not fret. Be about spreading My love. I am counting on you. My Heart is so sad for My hurting ones. I am talking to you. If you hold back, no one hears the treasure I have given to you. Speak for I am with you. I am doing the work. You are My vessel to reach many. Do not hold back! This trip is for their recovery. Give them My love letters. I need you to speak. Holding back is hurting My aching Heart. I want you to spread this this day. Be aware and ever ready. Do not ignore your children. They need you to talk to them about Me. The seeds you plant here will germinate for I will tend to them with My loving care. Oh, child, how I love My beloved ones. Tell them, tell them! Their hearts are aching and I have love to give them. Nothing fills the starved soul but the love of God.

You search, you wander, you roam and where do you go? Go to My loving arms! Oh, I await you with such love and joy. My arms are open, My Heart is on fire. I am the Sacred Heart of Jesus. I am your Savior. I am your all. I am He Whom you seek. Come to Me and open wide your hearts, look into My eyes, feel My touch. I am not a God far off. I am here this very day. I am in your midst.

You are My beloved ones. Oh, beloved of My Father, that I would give My life for you and you do not see your preciousness yet. You wander, you roam. Look at yourself, a creation of My Father! You are truly blessed. You were created by the hand of the Father.

You were made His beautiful ones, given all the beautiful things you need to do His work. You are precious. You are so full of such beautiful treasures. Praise Him Who created you! Do as He wills, lead the souls of many to His Holy Kingdom. The souls of your brothers are at stake. Your speech, your actions, your love may be the determining factors that lead them home. Your work is laid out before you. Do not give in to the promptings of the evil one to get you bowed down. Be the light that shines in the darkest night. Be My amber to this dark world. I am Jesus, I am your love. You are My precious ones. Come to Me and let Me love you. I will give you such love that you can scarcely speak and you, My beloved ones, will radiate My love to this cold world. Love Me, love one another. This and this alone is what I ask.

Be the light that shines in the darkness. Be the warmth to the cold heart. Everything should be rooted in Me and My love. Love God, love one another. I am the Sacred Heart of Jesus. I am on fire for love of you. I am Who am. Come to Me, My little, scared ones, and I will give you all you need! I love you!

April 24, 1994   5:00a.m.
Be at Peace—I Lead You

Come to Me, My sweet one. I am waiting for you to be with Me. Do not feel bad, as if you have done something wrong. Promote My love at every minute. Do not be afraid to speak out for My love. Time is so short, My beloved one. Time is wasting while you hold back. Do not fear. Where are you going?

Do not be anxious for your prayers. Be at peace. I will lead you. You must follow. Be at peace here. Be to this world as one in love. You are in love with Me. I know you miss Me. Operate only for love of Me, not to promote yourself. Things will unfold as I plan them.

Live only for love of Me. What comes from your mouth will be natural. You only live for My love and love Me ardently. Do not be angered or anxious. This is not from Me. My way is peace and love. Love your children. Play and pray with your children. Be alone with them.

I am Jesus. I am the Son of God. Be at peace. I love you so. All will work in the right time. Talk to those I send to you. I love you,

My sweet one. Be at peace. Do not fret or fume for anything. I care for you. I love you. I am yours. I love you always.
Your beloved Jesus. I love you!

April 24, 1994 After Communion 8:00p.m.
You Shed Your Blood for All

Note: I saw an inner vision in my heart so clearly and felt it.

R. I see Your blood, so red and so thick. It is by Your blood that we are saved. You shed Your blood for us—red and thick, real human blood. Oh, Jesus, You are so good to us to give Your very own blood.

Oh, Lord, I love You. I love You so much. Please, Lord, let me feel Your presence. Let me feel You more alive within me. I see Your blood, so red and so thick. It makes it so real to me. This is the cup of salvation. You gave Your very last drop of blood for us. You, God, did this for us. How can I not meditate on this? You shed Your very own blood for me. Oh, Jesus, I love You so. I want to do what You call me to do. I am weak. I am worldly. I am so full of self. How do You love me so with all these faults. You loved me so to shed Your blood. I see it so thick and so red. It makes it so real to think of it streaming, so thick and red, from under Your thorns, down Your cheeks and into Your eyes and Your ears. And You chose to do this, Jesus, because You loved me.

Oh, Jesus, I love You so! You are so good. I do not even know You yet. I want to know You and love You more and I know so little. My heart aches to know You more. I yearn from my chest to know You. Please tell me more of Yourself. Open me and let me experience more of You, Lord. I love You so. I want to tell all of Your Passion and death. I want to read Your letters and tell them how You bled such deep red, thick, real blood just for them. You gave Your very own blood for love of us.

Oh, Jesus, Jesus, I see Your blood so clearly, beading. This makes Your sufferings so real to me. Oh, Jesus, You Are real. You were a real, live, human being, and You were God, yet You gave Your very blood, Your very life, for love of me and for love of each and every person individually.

Oh, Jesus, You did this for my dear brothers. You loved them so much You shed Your blood for them. Teach me more how to love those You love. I love with such reservations. You love with no reservations. To Your death You gave Your all for me and my brothers. Who am I not to see their preciousness, that You loved them so much that You died for them? Teach me to love those You love, all my brothers, to realize You shed Your red, thick blood for them.

Oh, Jesus, I see Your blood, so thick and red, when they pierced Your head with thorns—because the head really bleeds—but You bled so! I wonder how much You had left after all of Your lesions. Oh, Jesus, You gave it all—thick, red blood. You gave every drop for love of us. You held nothing back until Your very death. You shed it all, all You had, for love of me. Teach me to love, Lord, to love those You shed Your very own blood for. Who am I to love some and not some? You loved us all to Your very death. Oh, Jesus, I have so far to go to know You and Your ways. I come to You with longing and burning in my chest. The more I know You, the more I cannot even fathom You. You are so beautiful, so perfect! You are my Savior, my lover, my precious Jesus. You are God and You shed Your blood for me. Oh, Jesus, such dignity and honor and worth You gave to us! Take my life. I am Yours, Lord. I love You so. I want to spread Your love. I am, oh, so weak! Show me Your way.

I am Yours!

I love you so, My child. You cannot even imagine a small amount of My love. Focusing on My Passion teaches you a little of My love. I would die for you, dear one, this very day. Just for you! I would shed every drop of blood. I would go through every pain. I would endure all My suffering for you today. I love you so. Be with Me. Stay with Me. Pray with Me. I await you, My beloved. I am truly present in the Eucharist. It wounds Me so to love you so much and be ignored. I have all you need. I have all you will ever need. I am Jesus Christ, the Son of God. I am your beloved Jesus. Oh, I love you, child. Preach My love, please. My beloved ones are suffering. You have the key to their life. It is the ardent, on-fire love of Jesus. this day preach My love to all your brothers. I love them so.

I died for you. Do you even realize? Do you think about My death and that I gave My life for you? It is in meditating on My Passion that you receive a golden reward. You learn so much from My Passion and death. Contemplate My walk with Me. Feel My agony. Know the way. Walk it with Me and you will know My great love for you. You will never know My love until you meditate on My Passion. It is there you know Me so well. You will learn so much from this study. Pray the sorrowful mysteries. Walk the way of the cross. I came and shed My blood for you. I would do it this very day.

Oh, My beloved ones, when will you turn to Me for that which you seek? Search you a barren desert, read you empty books! Come to Me and stay with Me after you receive the Eucharist. I will teach you such profound knowledge. Come to Jesus, sit in front of My tabernacle. I know all things. I will teach you the real things you need to know. I am Jesus, the Son of God. I am your love.

I am the Way, the Truth and the Life. You search, you seek, you find nothing. You are empty inside. When will you quit trying, trying to get more of what gives you only emptiness? I give you what you need. You go to empty closets. You keep searching in more empty closets. You never find anything. What do I tell you? I give you manna from heaven. You keep looking for your answers in a world that will vanish before your eyes. Your treasures are so momentary. You find nothing, yet you keep searching. You would think you would get the message, but you try even harder. Do you get it?

I am the Way, I am the Truth, I am the Life. If you want life, you come to the source. You seek, you wander, you find emptiness, yet you seek more emptiness. I am the Way. I am the only Way. You search, you seek in vain, you find absolutely nothing that gives you what you need. I am your all. Come to Me. Let Me feed you manna from heaven. I am Jesus. I am your all. I am the Son of God. Harken and be filled by Me!

April 24, 1994

Jesus, Our Innocent Lamb

R. I was so filled with intense sorrow during the Mass when the priest talked about the innocent lamb led to the slaughter. I could see Jesus, totally silent, in His humbleness, being led and suffering. It was awful.

Then today, on Mt. Krizevac, at the eleventh station, thinking of them nailing His hands was so much I could hardly take it. I wanted to cry from such sorrow and scream because of the sadness. To do that to Jesus! I couldn't stop sobbing. I love Him so much and He loves us so much. To think of them putting nails in his hands and nails in His feet is awful!

The little, Innocent Lamb! Then I saw his blood. I didn't see it, I see it so strong in my heart and I feel the emotions so strong because I love Him so much and He loves everyone so much to do this and they do not know or even think about Him. Such pain, to know this and watch the blind world.

Oh, Jesus, I love You so. I want to do whatever You ask to spread Your love, but how, how do I do it? I am willing to do whatever You ask. I live for You, my Lord. I love You so!

See Each Person As a Gift from God

My child, do not fret or fume. Take this message for My beloved ones. When I died on the cross, I held not back. I, God, gave My all for you that you might be saved. I loved you so much. No one knows the things I tell you. I tell you with My emotion and tenderness. You must preach My intense love. No one will know how I am telling you. I let you experience some of My sadness and My suffering. I love you intently. All can have this intimacy with Me and know Me as a Person. They must spend time with Me in front of the tabernacle.

Do not be attached to any person, place or thing. You are here to promote My love and My love alone. Do not ever worry or fret. Turn every moment over to Me. Realize that each moment is only as it brings you closer to Me. Your job is very important to Me. You must live only for love of Me. Forget little details. Live only to promote My love. If your brother comes to you, help him, pray for My help and answer as I do in you. Nothing is a coincidence.

Pray the Prayer for Union with Me all day. Your greatest satisfaction should come from loving Me and your brothers. Spend time talking to your children about Me today. See each person as a gift given from God and love them. When you have any interaction with them, love them as I would. This is your calling from Me: to love your brothers. They are so dear to Me, each precious child. Tell them how I love them, how indeed precious they alone are to Me.

Pray to see with the eyes of God. I see not their bodies. I see not their money. I see them as the beautiful persons they are and I love them. If they are acting nastily, love them anyway. See them with the eyes of God. They were created with such specialness by My Father. No other person can take their place in My Heart. Lead your brothers back to Me with your love.

Love everyone. Do not love some and ignore some. They are all My precious ones! So you look, you see their hair, their clothes, their money. Don't do this, My beloved ones. See the creation of the God Who lives within them. See them as My precious ones for whom I died on the cross. I gave My blood that they might live. I want them to be drawn to My Sacred Heart. I died for them, too. How can you size up people and then cast them off? See with the eyes of God. Pray to love all your brothers. You cannot do this alone. I do not call you to a select membership into your club of friends. I call you to be brothers in Christ. You are all brothers. No one is to be excluded because of their skin color or their bank account. I call you, My beloved ones, to love of your brothers. If you love Me, you will love all your brothers.

You pray for the gift to love all with the eyes of God. Tend to your brothers. They are hurting. I call you, little ones, to love. I call you to act as I would act. Gentleness, kindness, love—no exclusion of any person! Be kind and loving to My beloved ones for Me. I shed My last drop of blood for them. Will you do this? Hard, you say. Love, I say. I see with the eyes of God. I do not see the gold. I do not see the self that glories in itself. I see the beautiful creature, created uniquely by the hand of My Father. I see that person as loved by Him and loved by Me and the Holy Spirit. I see the child that is mothered by My very own mother. I see your brother and I ask you to love your brother. If you love Me, you will love your brothers. How can you love Me, Whom you do not see, if you cannot love your brothers, whom you see?

Pray to love with My Heart. You cannot do it alone.

R. I say, "But Lord, I have to protect myself and my children," and He says, "You have to love. I will protect you. Your loving your brother may be the very thing that saves his soul. It is no little thing I call you to. It is essential. If you love Me, you will love your brothers. You will not love some. You will love all. Pray to see with My eyes. You are so blind! You see the exterior of your brothers. See the soul that needs to get to heaven! Preach My gospel by your love. Are you preaching the gospel that I do not like some of your brothers and cast others off, that I do not give them passes into My club of friends. I love them, each precious child created by My Father."

"You will know they are Christians by their love." Do you love all your brothers? "But," you say, "Jesus, I just don't want to" and I say, "How can you say you love Me when I am calling you to this and you refuse Me and go about your stiff-necked ways?" You turn your head to some and turn your head from others. Oh, little ones, pray for My grace to love. Pray for My grace to see your brothers as your brothers in Christ. You spend half your life sizing up your friends and admitting them into your little club. I want all to read this message. You are all members of My club. You are My precious ones. Remember, you waste half your life letting some people into your circle and pushing others out of your circle. You do not even know how to love. You do this automatically. You don't want to love all your brothers. You want to love only the ones you let in. I call you to love your brothers. I gave the last drop of My blood for them, remember this! You spend much time in useless tasks, keeping track of how you have been offended, keeping track of who is accepted and who isn't. Then you call yourself Christ-like!

You must look to Me for your lessons on being Christ-like. I love every single person. I love every soul today. I would die for each precious one today. I exclude no man. You waste so much time doing senseless tasks that are so unloving. Pray to have Me open up your hearts. You do not even know how you offend Me. Pray to be Christ-like. Pray to love as I call you to love. Love is the key. You will learn to love from Me and Me alone. Come to Me and let Me open your hearts to the love of God. There is no club. You are all My chosen ones. I would die for each of you. I shed My blood for your brothers. Love them, all of them!

See With the Eyes of God

Note: Birds were chirping, roosters were crowing and there was light around Our Lady.

R. "And forgive us our trespasses, as we forgive those who trespass against us." But I had reservations in my heart. I look with the eyes of disapproval on my brothers I do not even know. I size you up, my brother. I judge. I think I know why you should not be loved by me. Is this the devil, to not love someone I don't even know? How many times have I sized people up to see how truly beautiful they were. Oh, the eyes of man and the eyes of God! Do I reach with the eyes of God or am I stiff-necked and looking the other way, not even knowing why I turn my head from you, my brother? Are you old or small, or do I just look and don't like you? Are your clothes different from mine, your hair too thin, too puffy? Why did I decide you weren't my brother? Oh, Jesus, do I see at all?

Message from Mary
I Suffered with Him

I am Mary, your mother, child. I am here. I love you and I mother each precious child. I love my beloved ones so. Do you not love your brothers, the same little ones that I mother? I am your mother. I am their mother. You are all my children! Love your brothers. Pray to be Christ-like, turn to my Son. He is the Way, He is the Truth, He is the Life. The life He gives to you. Come to Him. He has all you need. I am your mother. Thank you for responding to my call, my little children.

I am the Immaculate Heart. I love you with My tender Heart. I heard the blows they gave to my own and I could scarcely look up. I heard the blows, the awful blows. My Son stood in silence while they hit Him.

I could scarcely stand to walk the way with Him. I was so sick at what they had done, but I wanted to be with my Son. I walked by the grace of God.

They hung Him on the cross. I was so weak I could barely stand. I was held up by John. I watched my Son in such agony. Oh, my beloved Son! What had He done to deserve such agony. He loved you to His death. He was crucified for love!

April 25, 1994
I Call You to Do My Will—Do You Answer?

R. I can't judge what His Will is for me by your behavior. I have to decide what He is calling me to do by whatever He is saying to me. If the whole world does one thing but He is telling me something else, I have to do His Will. You have your commands to follow from Him; I have mine.

If you choose to do something, but He tells me to do something else, I cannot get angry at you. I must love you where you are and pray for you. I am not the judge; I am not the jury; I am to spread His love. Always love nothing short of how He loved all. He did not condemn. He spoke about love; He spoke the truth. He is the Way, He is the Life, He is the Truth. His truth He makes known to us in His word, in our hearts, in these letters. I can choose His way or my own way. His ways He makes clear.

It is up to me to choose my will or His Will. Doing His Will is His Will. Many times it is not doing what I like at first, but He knows exactly what I need. Doing His Will is the way to live in harmony. He knows all things. Do I pick and choose and do my will or His Will? I know what He is calling me to do. Maybe I don't like it.

Writing these letters will not make me popular. Many do not want to love as He asks, give up their food, give up their pleasure, love everyone, even people they don't want to love, stop getting angry, get rid of self. "Oh," you say, "what fun is that?"

Put Aside Your Willfulness

That, My child, is what I ask. I ask you to follow Me. My way is not the way of the world, My way is the way to eternal life. I am the Way. I am the Truth. I am the Life. He who abides in Me will have eternal life.

Fear not, fret not, do My Will. I call you to obedience. I call you to love, not as you see love, loving those whom you please, being angry and holding on to grudges, holding on to pleasures that you do not need. This is not love of Me or love of My beloved ones! I call you to being Christ-like, holy as a saint, living life as I want you to live it, not as you want to live it. The war on this earth will only be fought with surrender and love, surrendering yourself and loving as I teach you to love. You are so willful! You do your own will and then tell yourself you are serving Me. Serving Me is doing My Will. It is acting in My ways. It is love, real love of God and love of one another. Love is not selfish, love does not seek its own way, love gives to the other. I call you to love. This demands selflessness and studying My ways. Oh, come to Me after Communion and in front of the tabernacle. I want to teach you this very day. Your time is borrowed. I lend it to you. All works out when you spend an hour with Me.

You are so willful. You want My time I lend to you. You do not want to spend an hour with Me. That is why you don't. You don't want to sit after Communion. My way is the only way. Listen and be taught or do your own thing and reap the benefits of doing what you want.

I am God. I call you to put aside your willfulness and open your hearts to My way. My way I make clear in front of the tabernacle and after Communion. Will you be willful or do My Will. I call you. Do you answer?

He Is So Close to Us

Do not worry, My sweet one. Time is short until I come. I am coming soon. I am He Who comforts you. Do not worry, for you have nothing to fear. I tend to your every need. I love you so, My little one.

R.I have been experiencing lots of visions but do not see Him, but I do. He walked all around Dubrovnik after Communion, until we ate lunch, wearing a white tunic and red garb. He was there talking to me the whole time. My chest burned so! On the deck next to the water, He kept talking.

Father S____ said the rosary on the bus to Dubrovnik. He made up meditations on the sorrowful mysteries. I had so much sorrow, I cried so hard, I couldn't pray. I just let myself feel the pain. It was an emotional experience, but such closeness to my precious Jesus!

This was some day for closeness to Him. He talked to me a lot all day. When I had doubts, He comforted me. It was so beautiful!

M____ gave me a book on purgatory. The letters said exactly the same as my letters. She told Father S____ she saw Jesus in the tabernacle.

I saw Jesus yesterday, a little lamb led to the slaughter, such a humble, beautiful face. I cried during Mass.

Nails in the hands...saw it...Blood on the head...beaded! I love Him so much, so close to Him...I experienced Him so alive...I saw Him in a white tunic on our bus...I really know He is here...visions in my heart and He talks to me...I say something to myself and He answers me so sweetly and affirmingly...such a beautiful day...I love Him so much...

At St. Blaze Church

Father S____ talked about all the crosses in Medjugorje and how we have to take up our cross and the way to Jesus is the way of the cross. Beautiful!

Such closeness after Communion, both days. I just sat there and wanted to stay forever.

April 27, 1994

My Way Is the Cross

R. Dear Jesus, I know You are present. I do not want to get up, but I love You so much. I am sorry I kept trying to sleep.

My messages are not just for you. Yesterday you did not have time alone with Me. I want to be alone with you. My messages are messages for each of My precious children. Feel My presence even though you do not see Me.

You are realizing how truly far you are from Me. I call you to holiness and sainthood. My way is not the way of this world. My way is the way of the cross. I ask you to sacrifice when you do not want to. I ask you to love your brother who is not so nice. I ask you to be Christ-like. Study Me and My Passion. To know Me, you must study Me and My suffering. I ask you to live for Me, to take up your crosses and live for Me. I call you to mortify yourself, to be cheerful about it and to show My love and gentleness to all. I call you, My child, to sainthood.

You say, "Oh, but I get no pleasure?" I say My love is your pleasure! You live to love Me. Be united to Me. No worldly thing can give you any gratification as My love. You must give it up willingly and with such love. I will pour My love into your soul.

You will feel My presence in a new way. I am truly by your side. You do not need your senses to see Me. I plant Myself in your heart. Reach, in all things, to know Me in your heart. I am truly present. Open wide your heart and let Me rest there with you. I am truly your best friend. Do you want to know Me? Relinquish all your cares here and make Me first. Live for My love.

Love Me, sweet one. I long for you and your love. Come to Me with such eagerness. Think of Me at every second. Be united to Me in a way you have never known. Feel My presence by your side. Think of My love for you to lay down My life for you and suffer such a brutal death. I am truly your love. The cross is your comfort. Carry your cross and hold it close to your heart. It is My sign of My immense love. You should find such comfort holding the cross. I gave My life for you.

When you hold the cross, you know how immensely you are loved. The cross is your comfort, not your enemy. I came that I might give you life. It is through the cross that you are saved. Hold the cross all night in bed. Carry it so closely to your heart. You are instantly comforted thus. You do not fear, you do not fret, you behold the cross of Christ and you live in His love given for you. It is in My blood that you are saved. I gave Myself, body and blood, that you would live.

I want your all. I do not want you to hold back. I want you to be so closely united to Me. Surrender yourself entirely. Give up the little things that hold you bound and you will be freed into My immense love. The price you pay is nothing for the gift you receive. I am that Person you felt truly by your side yesterday. Focus on My presence. I am with you every minute. I am loving you. You are never alone. Not for an instant do I leave your side.

You leave Me for your little whims. You take your eyes off Me. You go to your world. You hope that you will find some pleasure. You find momentary pleasure, only to be left more hungry. I and I alone feed your hungry soul. You thirst a barren desert and I am by your side.

Little one, little one, you are holding yourself bound to this world. Let go and fall into My waiting arms. I never ever leave you. I am truly by your side. Feel My presence. Reach with the soul.

Picture Me clothed in white and red and being with you as you walk.

Oh, sweet one, I am there. It is you who do not see because you do not want to let go. Let go, surrender all to Me. Let Me go with you where you go. Go you never alone. I am by your side with such love!

I love you. I am Jesus. Come and be with Me in the Eucharist and in the tabernacle. I am waiting for you there in such a special way. I am your God. I love you. I never abandon you. I long for your love and your closeness. Let Me embrace you. I embrace you in your surrender. Our union depends on your selflessness and surrender to Me. Let Go. Be constantly with Me. Know Me, love Me, make Me your all.

I am Jesus, the Son of God. Let go. I love you. Jesus.

April 27, 1994
My Father Created Your Brother

How much time do you waste, My child, sizing yourself up? Do you ask yourself how you are being admired by those around you? How much time do you spend worrying what others are thinking? Think of how you worry about how you are doing. Then you look at your brothers to see how you like them. How are they doing? Do you see them with human eyes or do you see them with My eyes? I do not see your hair. I do not see all the exterior things you think are so important. I see My beloved ones!

Do you see how your thoughts are being used for such unloving things? You do not have to size up your brothers. You need to love them. You waste your time when you could be loving My beloved ones. You do unloving things you do not even know.

My Father created you so special. See your specialness. Become selfless. Live only for love of God and love of one another. Such freedom! Your time is not your own. Why do you squander it so? Why do you think such senseless things are so important? I ask you for two things: love of God and love of one another.

I must be the center of your existence. All your moments must center around your love for Me. What do you think? What did he think? Who cares? Just focus on Me and My love. You are living to love Me. This earth is a transit place to another place. Do you not try, when you are on the bus, to do everything to reach your destination? This is not your destination. This is only the way you use to get to heaven. Keep always before your eyes your real goal. See the end as the end, not the moments you are living here.

I am the Way, the Truth, the Life. You follow My way, you live My truth. I give you life, not as this world wants life, but life eternal.

Do not waste your precious thoughts. Operate for love of Me. I am Jesus. I am your God. You must always focus on My love and love those whom I love. I love your brothers. Love them for Me. I loved them to My death.

I am your all. Come to Me and I will give you rest. Clean your heart of any impurities. Your heart must be pure in My ways. I want you holy like saints.

Strive for Peace Within

I am your precious Jesus. I want to deliver a message for the world. I want you to concentrate on peace. Do you have peace in your own heart? How can you show peace to this world if you do not hold peace within yourself.

Strive for interior peace. You, of yourself, cannot do this. You need My help to see you through. You must ask for help to carry out My task. The interior peace will flow to your brothers in all you do. Strive to be at peace inside. If you live for love of Me, you will find this peace.

Remain selfless. Do not promote yourself in anything. You are living to spread My love. Do not ever fight or argue. Live in silence. I will take care of you. Turn all cares over to Me. I am your Savior and I love you.

Live in peace. I give you peace. I am Jesus, peace is up to you. You must strive for this peace within. I love you.

I could find no other seat but in front of the bus. Jesus said:

I provided the seat. Now you read the message.

I read the tabernacle message, kept praying, hoping I wouldn't have to ask to read it, but He said:

Do it for love of Me. If you do not speak, no one will hear. I provided the seat. You read the message.

Don't Judge the Father's Beautiful Creation

R.He said in church at Mass that, if I look at the exterior of my brothers and size them up, I am judging God the Father's beautiful creation. The person has nothing to do with his skin color, his height, his hair color, his whatever. He was created by God the Father as he is. Jesus died and shed His blood for each and every person. Who are we to decide we don't like what God the Father created?

He said (similar to the talents letter of Oct. 3, 1993) that we have nothing to do with our talents, that they are given by God to do the work He has planned for us. To be envious of our brothers is sinful. The message is so beautiful.

To look at someone and say, "Boy, what a big nose" is to criticize the Father's creation. We are to love God. If we are criticizing his creation, this is not good. He could have given us a nose that would be so big. I didn't have anything to do to get my nose. Who am I to be so proud that mine is better than yours when they were both created by the Father?

April 29, 1994

I Give You the Key to Conquer Satan

I am the Alpha, I am the Omega, I am your loving Savior come to this earth to save you. I send you these hand-delivered messages to help hurting souls. Look around you at the souls that need these messages. I am your loving Savior. I died for you. I am begging you to help (her) to get them out. Every day souls are being lost because they are not being taught about My love. She is My messenger. She needs to speak. She needs to tell all of these messages.

I love My beloved ones so very dearly. Please help get these messages to My loved ones. So many are hurting so badly! Love of God, love of one another!

Satan is working so hard to divide your workers. They need these messages about love and anger. Please see that they get this message. I love them so dearly. My renewal will come from the Center. Satan wants to divide your beloved workers. Publish these letters on love and anger. Your flock is hurting and needs to know My love and operate from love of one another. Your city will be lit only by the love of God. Read these messages on love this week. They need to circulate. Satan wants you divided. I am giving you the key to help them conquer his cunning. Love of God, love of one another! I love you so. You are My beloved servant.

Thank you for listening. I love you!

April 29, 1994   **6:30a.m.**

I Have All the Power

Dear child, do not fume, do not fret. Hold tight to all I have taught you. You will know peace if you listen to My teachings. Satan wants to trip you up. He has no power over you! You must stay fixed on Me and My love. I love you so intently! I am Jesus Christ, the Son of God. I love you. Why should you worry about anything on this earth?

I am He Who has all the power and I am guarding your way. The devil uses your thoughts to taunt you. Focus your thoughts on Me and loving Me. Do not judge your brothers or worry what they think of you. Operate from love of Me and from selflessness. I will make things happen.

Obey Me in everything I make clear to you in your heart. Be open and focused constantly on Me. I guard your way. Concentrate on My Passion and how I loved you to My death and love you this way this very minute.

I, God, loved you to My death, child. Your only concern is love of Me and love of one another. Strive to love and bring others to heaven.

I call you to preach the gospel this day in your being. Do not miss an opportunity to be Me to this world.

I love you. I go with you. My way is peace. You have nothing to fear ever. I am by your side. I love you, My beautiful child. Come to Me and you will find rest. I operate you and you can rest in My arms. Let go, surrender. I am truly here. I love you. Jesus.

April 29, 1994 On a plane from Rome
Think of Me

My dear child, do not worry who sees you writing. I want you to write when I tell you to. You are My instrument to reach many. If the whole world does something else, you do as I tell you to. this day you must focus on My love. Put all thoughts of judgment aside and just think of Me. I am calling you to such union with Me.

I am your ardent lover. I love you so.

April 30, 1994   5:00a.m.
Do Not Fear—I Walk with You

R.My heart is full of such fear, Jesus. I place all my trust in You.

I am with you, My beloved one. Breathe in Jesus, breathe out fear. I have not gone from your side. Let go and give yourself to Me. I am the Alpha, I am the Omega. I am Who am. I will handle whatever you need. Letting go is what I ask you to do. Let go of it all, My little one. You do not let go and you are left empty. You let go and fall fastly into My waiting arms.

Place all your trust in Me. Hold My crucifix, meditate on My Passion. I am Jesus, Son of the Living God. I will care for all your worries. Let go and surrender. Do not talk personally about yourself. Do not talk about anything but the messages. I love you dearly.

Let go into My arms. No one has the gift you have. I am giving you these letters My way. You hurt My aching Heart to be given such a gift and to give in to Satan's prompting you to doubt. Fear and doubt are Satan's playground. Go to the unknown. I am by your side. You do not know where you are going, but you will live in My love. I will care for you minute-by-minute. Each day you surrender leads you to My waiting arms. Fear not for anything. A band of angels is by your side. You must focus on the unseen world. The fear you experience now will teach you such a lesson! How do you learn without such crosses? You are loved so much - beyond your belief. I do not get mad at you. I love you despite your imperfections. I am the teacher; you are My pupil.

You are My beloved one, created by the Father. Dispel the darkness and walk into the light. Warmth and security surround you and you go hand in hand with Me into the world.

April 30, 1994

Love All I Send to You

R. I do not pick the people He puts in my path. He puts people in my path and they may not be of my choosing. I must realize He is in charge of all things. He wants me to touch certain people. I do not get to pick whom He sends. Do they fit in my club? Then I will lead them to Christ.

He loves all of our brothers. He knows whom He wants us to touch. It is His Will, not mine. I am the empty vessel He uses.

Let go, My child. Let it happen. Let Me use you as I desire. Do not close doors to people I send to you. I know far better than you who needs to be loved by Me through you. You size up the person. You will help this one, not talk to that one. No, no, My little ones. Be the empty vessel I use. Let it happen! Do not be in a huff to help him and not the old, thin lady. The old, thin lady is the one who needs My love this day. Did you say "no" when I sent her to you? I am asking for your surrender and your selflessness. I am asking you to be the empty vessel I use. I will send My beloved ones to you for My love. You must be open and love all your brothers. Get rid of your preconceived ideas. Look with the eyes of God. See in each child the precious creation of God the Father.

Pray for selflessness, little, beloved one. Oh, I want you to love for Me! Be open and ready to love all your brothers. I am Jesus, Son of the Living God. I live in you. Be My open door. Love for Me. They will never know My love if you love only those you choose. I know who needs Me. Open up, child. When I send you a beloved child of

My Father, be ready and eager to love that child. Look with the eyes of God and see all My beloved ones. To My death I shed My blood for each and every soul. Who are you to criticize a creation of God the Father? When you love your brothers, short, tall, old, black, white, you love Me.

Turn Your Thoughts to Love

R. I felt His presence, saw Him plainly in my heart, wearing a white tunic, standing by the tabernacle. He was truly present. I saw His beautiful, brown hair and gentle face. He waits for you, little ones. He is waiting for you to come and share yourself with Him, to just sit and be with Him Who loves you dearly and Whom you love. Feel the warmth in your chest, for He, the Son of God, truly stands here waiting for you. He is present. See Him waiting for you.

Do you love Me as I have loved you? Are you willing to lay down your life for Me? Would you give your life rather than deny Me or put anything before Me? I call you to holiness. I call you to follow Me, the Master. I loved you to My death. Do you love Me first, that you would die for love of Me? Do you love your brothers as I have loved you? Would you die for your brothers because I ask you to love them this way?

You do not know how to love. I tell you, but you do not listen because you do not want to love as I have loved you. Loving as I have loved is not easy. It is simple but difficult. I love you this way this day. Love, My children. Love is the answer. Love is nothing as the world preaches. Look at Me dying on the cross. I teach you how to love. I held not back one thing for love of you.

Do you want to love? Study Me and My Passion. Carry the crucifix by your side. Look at Me. I teach you how to love.

You preach My love in your very being. Are you preaching My giving love to all your brothers? I am Love. Follow My way. Love as I showed you how to love.

I am Jesus. Love, love, love. Do not have unloving thoughts. Take your thoughts and turn them to love, love of God, love of one another. I love you, My dear ones. I love you. I remain in the tabernacle. Come and be with Me, My ardently loved ones.

I never ever leave your side. Let go, little one. You are on a pilgrimage in My world and I am the leader. I care for you with such love. You have no fears. I never leave you unattended. I guard you. I watch you. I live in you and you carry My love to this world. Say the Prayer for Union with Me.

Until the ends of this earth I never leave you. Surrender to Me. The devil will really work on you in your tiredness. I go with you. My lady is by your side. You are being led and watched by God— Father, Son, Holy Spirit—and the Blessed Mother, angels and saints. Fear not, child. This is a fact. You must trust and have faith in the God Who loves you.

I am your God. I love you, My little baby. Let Me care for you with such love!

Love God, Love One Another

Where do My children go in their busy lives? People are so hard in the face. They are irritable, they push around so quickly. Where are they going? There is no peace in their faces, in their hearts, in their lives. Where do they go? What are they doing? In one second I could snatch their life and it is over!

How did you love? Nothing matters except how you loved Me and loved your brother. I call you to love of him, yet you treat him so cold. You tell your brother to get out of your way and you move stone-jawed ahead. You are in a hurry.

Think of an anxious bird. "Oh, how silly," you say. "A bird that is hurried and has to move quickly ahead?" "Oh, so silly," you say? You are just as silly with your anxiousness. I tend to the birds of the air. I tend to much more. I tend to you, My beloved ones.

I call you to love. I call you to kindness. I call you to be Christ-like. What is your gauge for living? Do you live to please Me or live to please yourself? Is your self ever satisfied? Does it say, "Now I feel good"? The self searches for that which only I can provide. The soul of each person craves the love of God. Without God in your heart there is misery. Your degree of happiness is proportional only to how you love God and your neighbor.

Seeking the self is misery. The self is never satisfied. It wants more and more and is satisfied less and less. Where are you going in your busy lives? How did you love? How did you love God and love your brothers?

Are you miserable? The world leaves you hard and empty. The world leaves you in a state of misery, of want for more, but never having enough. The world begs you to satisfy yourself and robs you of the love of God. I call you to selflessness. The world demands selfishness.

Oh, My precious ones, as quick as a summer rain I come and call your soul home to Me. My way is the way of love. When I call, will you have stored up treasures of love for Me and your brothers or will you have an empty heart?

I fill your heart with love. Only I can give you the love you seek. You search, you wander, you roam, while I wait here for you with an endless source of love and peace and joy. I fill your heart to the brim. The world robs you of your joy. It makes you self-seeking and you never find any joy there.

I am the Way. I am the Truth. I am the Life. I am Jesus, Son of the Living God, and I come to you this day with such love. Will you come and get your supplies? You are My soldiers in an empty world. You are the hearts full of the love of God. You will minister to My hurting ones for Me. You are My love given to your brothers. Will you answer My call to you to be a soldier in My army? Nothing you do here matters if it is not rooted in love. I am God and I am Love. I am the source of your joy. Come to Me, My babies. I give you all you need. I give you peace, joy and love.

I fill the aching heart and it operates in this world with love. Look at your stiff-necked brothers. See their pain. It is your love for them that will reflect the God within your soul. Oh, they know you are Christians by your love. Be Christ-like. Dismiss all hate and anger of your brother. Let your hearts be so pure, so full of My love! Come to Me. I wait for you, My loved ones. I await you in the tabernacle. I await you in the Holy Eucharist. Wherever you go, I go by your side. I am your God and I have loved you to My death. Will you love your brothers this way for Me.

May 2, 1994   **5:10a.m.**
Unite

Oh, My child, trust. I am indeed present to all at the Center. I am working in your hearts. You are all parts of the big picture. You must unite. All there must learn to love, not as they see love, but as I am teaching you to love. You do such unloving things and do not even know.

They need these letters on love at the Center. Love and union are what will make you light up the world. You must all learn to love. Put your hate, anger and sizing each other up aside. Unite. I am using each person there.

Prayer is the answer. Prayer is silence before Me in the tabernacle. I speak in your heart. Preach to others how to become open to My promptings in their hearts. Every person is needed. Every person has a part to play. Read these letters on love. Love is the key. Satan will divide you if you do not keep yourselves rooted in My love and strive for unity. I am communicating to all there. It takes time with Me after Communion and in front of the tabernacle. Pass out the little book and message on the tabernacle. Pass out the letters of love.

There cannot be strife and competition in your hearts. You are all called. How can you show the world about love when you do not know about love yourself? Love is the key that will light the city. Love is what you need to unite!

Satan wants to divide your workers. He wants them to compete and look with anger at each other. Know, My little ones, that he is constantly talking to you and trying to divide you. Love as I have loved you. Love your brothers. That is action, that is not "tolerance." That is not seeking self, that is giving self, that is being humble, that is mending fences, that is saying you are sorry, that is being in touch with Me. You cannot love without My graces. You need to be alone with Me. I speak to your heart in the silence. Stay after Communion. I, the Son of God, Jesus, Who died on the cross, long to be with you and give you all you need. Stay with Me, My beloved ones. I love you so much.

Do not look at your brothers and size them up. Pray for them to be drawn closer to My Sacred Heart. You are not doing this alone. Do you see in the confirmations, how you are all receiving My promptings? You cannot get My messages for you if you do not sit in silence with Me. I speak in the silence to you. I speak in the inner promptings of your heart.

You do not need to promote yourselves, you need to do My work. I am using you as a unit. Unite in love. Whenever any ill thoughts of your brothers come to your head, dismiss them and pray the Prayer for Union with Me. I know everything that is happening and I want My work accomplished. Let Me take care of your brother who is irritating you. I can do it far better than you could ever do it.

Love, this is your call. Love, union, forgiveness, saying you are sorry. This takes Me. You cannot do it alone. "But," you say, "I don't want to say I'm sorry." I say that is what mends the fence. It is like the nails that hold the boards. A humble, loving heart will hold it together. Do not be prideful. Pride is the downfall. This comes from focusing on yourself. Pray my Prayer for Union with Jesus. This will help you to become more selfless and united to Me. A soul that is striving for union with Me will be a loving soul. The best gift you can give this world is to be about your relationship with Me. I mold your heart. I dismiss your fear. I wash away anger and doubt and you come away with My love.

Love will light this city. You must tend to the pruning in your own hearts. Do not criticize your brother. Be loving and pray for him. Dismiss all hate and anger. It is not from Me. I operate in love. You can accomplish so much with love. Argumentation, belaboring the point, is from Satan.

Pray for each other. Pray for union with Me. Pray for the union of your brothers to My Sacred Heart. Lead all to silent prayer with Me. Read the Scriptures. Read these letters, letters of love from Me to My beloved ones! Oh, how I love! You do not know how to love. How can you love and teach others when you do not know yourself. Circulate the letters—on the tabernacle, hate and anger, and loving your brothers—at the Center. Give them to all who are the backbone of the operation. They need to love, love God, love one another. That will light your city. You will be on fire with the burning love of Jesus in your hearts. You cannot do it alone. You must come to Me.

I am the Alpha. I am the Omega. I am your God and I am doing My work through you. I am working. Make yourself selfless. I can do all things if you surrender yourself to Me. I love you. I want you to write music and songs. Jesus.

Teach Your Children My Love

I am inside of you. Read this letter to your children and their friends. I am Jesus Christ, the Son of God. At My name all knees should bend. In My presence you should be in awe and ardent devotion. I am Jesus. I want to be adored and worshiped. I want to be honored as God. Do you honor Me after Communion? I am God, child. Where do you rush in a hurry? To eat? Children need to spend time with Me. Do not teach them the bad habit of running for food. Tell them about My True Presence. Bring your breakfast and eat later. You have time. I want your time afterwards for 20 minutes. Teach the children this. They need to be alone with Me, too. I do not come to you and them in a different way. I am present, truly here. If they can spend 20 minutes with their best friend, they can spend 20 minutes with Me also. This is your opportunity to teach them a good lesson and not a bad one.

I am Jesus Christ, the Son of God. You are a tabernacle. Do not run from My altar to please the children. Teach them a lesson for life. Nothing compares to the time after Communion. God is in your breast. God, child! Do you hear Me? Nothing compares to God! I can do all things in My divinity and love. I come to you, a mere human, and you think you have to tend to worldly things. This offends Me so. You do not know. I come in love. Receive Me in love and reverence. Teach your children of My love.

Vision of Mary

R.The tenderness of Mary, holding the baby Jesus! See her as she looks so affectionately on her beloved Son, her eyes cast down in such love at her precious baby! See her as she holds the body of her Son after his brutal death on the cross. He is her beloved Son, the same beautiful baby she held. Now she looks with such love on Him Whom she once cared for as a baby.

Such sorrow, her Heart in such pain to behold her Beloved One on her lap! Pain, so intense that her Heart is pierced with a sword. Oh, Mary, Mary, I love you so. I thank you for all you suffered for us. You suffer for our sins because of all of your love for us and Jesus. I am sorry that I have made your suffering so much harder.

You, oh Mary, you, beloved mother, you mother us as you mothered Jesus. You mother us as babies and you mother us when we are suffering.

Message from Mary:

I cry for you, my child in your darkness. I cry for the beloved ones of my Son, Jesus. Turn their hearts back to His love. He is suffering for love of those in darkness. Turn their hearts to His intimate love. I am your mother and I thank you for responding to my call.

R.I see that lifeless body of Christ as she holds Him. This has been going on for a month. She holds Him. That must be the optimum of suffering, to hold your lifeless child in your lap, brutally beaten and crucified for loving. He had done nothing. Was this one of Mary's crucifixions? She suffered so! What of her suffering, her steadfastness to behold Jesus, always by His side, watching and suffering? Does Mary suffer by our side as we ignore her and continue to go our way and neglect her Son? She sees her Son and knows how He gave His life. She knows how He suffered. She knows it all, yet she has come and appeared. She begs us to return to Him. What more can she do to draw us to her Son?

What more can He do? He, God, died this brutal death!

How Mary suffered for love of us and love of Jesus!

Mary calls us to her Son. The Lady is calling on behalf of her beloved Son. She suffered the brutal passion, she heard the blows, she walked the walk only by the grace of God. She calls us to her Son. Will we answer?

Pray for Union with Jesus

Do not think of yourself and size yourself up in the eyes of man. You receive messages from Jesus Christ, the Son of God. Pray to only focus on the job at hand. You operate for love of Me. Do not waste your precious thoughts on making yourself look accepted in the eyes of man. Operate for love of God and you will treat men as you should. You waste such time sizing yourselves up and sizing up others. Love Me, Love your brothers. Do not give in to unloving thoughts. Operate only for love of Me.

Pray to be selfless. Pray, pray, pray, to die to self. This will keep you from pride. Pride is so powerful! It is the opposite of selflessness. It is a killer. It is a killer of the life and love of God that could exist in your heart. Do not evaluate yourself. Ask why you are acting. Are you acting to draw others to My love or are you acting to promote yourself? Pray for selflessness. Pray the Prayer for Union with Me. Do not give in to yourself. Discipline your thoughts. Pray for strength. Pray to be Christ-like. Pray for union with Me.

Do Not Worry

My dear child, what are you doing? Do not worry. Put all doubt aside and let Me comfort your heart. I am God. This life is very short. You do not focus on the things of this world.

Satan wants to get you focused on yourself always. Pray to be led by Me. Live for love of Me. Live only to draw all close to My Sacred Heart. Operate for love of your brothers. You will not become prideful or boastful if you constantly focus on bringing others close to Me. That is your goal, to draw others to My Sacred Heart, to tell them of My ardent love, to lead others to My arms. Your job is to promote the love of Jesus. Do not be smart in your speech. Be loving. Operate to draw others close to Me.

Do not be hurried. When someone approaches you, speak of My love. I am sending people to you. A few words from these letters can help a hurting soul. Do not focus on yourself at all. Focus totally on My letters to them. Love, love, love!

If you feel yourself getting irritated at your brother, pray for him and yourself. Pray to act Christ-like.

Do not be rushed. You are going nowhere. The love you give this day is all that matters. How did you preach the gospel in your being this day?

I am the Way. I am the Truth. I am the Life. I am your precious Jesus. Oh, how I love you, little one. Tell all how tender I am and how I wait for them and want to share Myself with them. I am the tenderest of hearts.

Mary is very close to you. She is so loving to her children! We are guarding your every move. Let go into the loving arms of Me and My mother. It is a fact that we are truly by your side, loving you and guarding you. Angels go where you walk. Pray to us constantly. We are always there.

Continue to focus on your union with Me. Pray the prayers, become selfless. You are not in this in any way to promote yourself. Constantly pray the Prayer for Union with Me. You must remain selfless or Satan moves in.

Let each day unfold. Do not be anxious. Let go. You are going nowhere. I am Jesus Christ, the Son of God, and I walk with you wherever you go. Feel My presence by your side, talk to Me, walk with Me. I am your best friend. Love Me, little one. I love you so and I want to be united to you. No human can be in union with you as I can. Let go and let it happen. Focus on Me and Me alone. You will love others when you are focused on Jesus. Love is from the heart. It is action. Do not hold back your emotions. Love Me, love your brothers!

Oh, how I love you, My sweet, little, beautiful children, created by My Father. You are His handiwork. Honor the creation the Father has made. Be loving to one another.

You are all His creations and I would die this day for your brothers. Guard your thoughts. Only think pure, loving thoughts. If you are troubled, pray. I will handle you and your problems. I love you so.

May 4, 1994   4:30a.m.
I Call You to Holiness

Dear ones, I am calling you to love your brothers. I have loved you. Would you, dear ones, lay down your lives for your brothers? How are you loving this day? Are you following Christ in your actions? I am the Way, I am the Truth, I am the Life. You must constantly put the world aside and look to the Master for all your directions. I call you, My little ones, to holiness. I call you to pure hearts, hearts that are full of love and empty of hate and anger. I call you to guard your hearts and watch that they stay forever holy. You, My precious bride, I want your soul white.

Do you criticize your dear brothers? I gave the last beat of My Heart and the last drop of My blood for the soul you are displeased with. I would die for them this day. Will you not love them for Me? They are so precious to Me!

Quit sizing up your brothers. You do such unloving things in your mind. You do not even know how unloving are your thoughts. You judge your brothers by their exteriors, by their education, by their money. You do not see the beautiful creation of God the Father. He created your brothers just perfectly and He loves His creation. Who are you to criticize His creation? Love your brothers when they are hurting. It is in your loving the hurting ones that they will see the reflection of Christ in you.

Do not hold on to foolish things. One moment and your days on this earth have ended. All that remains is how you loved. Did you love God? Did you love your neighbor? Love is not selfish. It gives of itself. Its whole purpose is to draw the other closer to Jesus.

Study the crucifix. It is such a comfort! I loved you so. I died for you. I would die for you alone this very day, little ones! Look at Me dying on the cross! The way to Me is to follow Me. Be Christ-like in your ways. You must study Me to know My ways. Do not give in to yourselves. My way is love. Will you be the reflection of the love of God within you? My way is the way of the cross. They persecuted Me, they hurt Me, they tore My flesh and spit on Me. They did this to Me for My love given to all! This world is not your end. You follow My ways and you move as you should toward your goal.

I am Jesus, I am the Son of God. I love you so ardently. I died and shed My blood, My beautiful blood, for love of you. I await you this day, My little ones. I loved you so I remain with you in the Eucharist. I await, I long for you to come and share in our love. I am the tenderest of Hearts. No man can be close to you as I. I love you so. I want to dwell and live within you. I want to fill you with all My love and radiate My love to your beloved brothers. I want to shine from your souls.

Oh, little ones, take Me seriously. I am truly here, begging for you to live in My love.

You are the light that will shine in this dark world. You will light up the darkest night with My love.

The best gift you can give to this world is to busy yourself about your love affair with Me. I love you, My little ones. I love you and I want to share this love with you.

Love your brothers. Do not let Satan talk in your heads and make them wrong and you right. Love them as I have loved you. Do not look at your brothers and size them up. See them with the eyes of God, the beautiful creations of the Father.

Will you love My beloved ones for Me this day, or will you say "no" to My call? Love your brothers in darkness. They need your love. I am calling you to love them for Me this very day. They may scoff at you and persecute you, but you will plant a seed that I Myself will water and give sunlight to. Plant seeds of love. This is the most important seed you will plant, a seed of love. Watch it grow as I provide it with water and nourishment. I will shine on your brothers through you if you stay in My love. Be the light that shines on this dark world. They are crying out for the love of God. They are suffering. They need your love.

Put yourselves aside. Die to yourselves. Live only for the love of God. If the world goes one way, you stay focused on My love. Do not follow the world. Follow the risen Christ!

I love you so, little ones. I bring you new life. I fill your hearts with My love. Pray to the Holy Spirit for His gifts. Pray the *Our Father.* Let My mother mother you as she mothered Me. She loved you so. She suffered so for love of you. She appears to bring you back to her beloved Son. Will you answer her call? She is calling you to put God first in your life. She is calling you to love, love of God, love of one another.

Forgive your brothers. Empty your hearts of hate and anger and let go. Let all your anger go. Give Me your resentments and let Me heal your hearts. Forgiveness is the way to peace. Let go. Do not size up your brothers. Love them all. Pray for them. Unite in My love. Love is a miracle cure. Say you are sorry. Be gentle in your ways. Pray for your needs. I love you, little ones. I am with you this day.

Will you answer the call and love for Me? I love you. I am your beloved Jesus. I would die this day just for you. I love you the same as I did the day I died. Turn to Me and give Me your life. I will care for you and love you. I am your Savior. I am Jesus Christ, Son of the Living God. Let Me live in your heart!

May 4, 1994 After Communion	7:10a.m.

Strive for Oneness

R. We are one body, one body in Christ. We are one in Him. He is one in us. This is the intimacy we have with Jesus. We become intimate with each other in our oneness with each other as we are joined in Christ. He is the vine, we are the branches. All who live in Him will bear great fruit.

Unite, My children, become one in Me. You must stay connected in My love. Strive for oneness. Satan is division. He wants to separate you. You cannot separate yourselves. We must be as one body.

Such intimacy you can achieve in Me! Strive for oneness with Me, and oneness with one another will follow. As you love Me, truly you, too, will love one another. Do not separate yourselves in any way from one another. Pray to be united, united in Me and My love. I died to bring you life. Stay one in Me and I in you. A body has many members. You must be one. Do not curse or shun one another. Be as your own body. You would not cut off your hand. The body functions when all its parts are working in harmony.

Unite, My beloved ones. Do not separate and hate each other. Love one another as I have loved you. I laid down My life, given freely for you. Love your brothers this way.

This life is so very short, here today, gone tomorrow. Nothing will be achieved if you separate. Love one another. Stay united in love. This is My command to you. All else is of no account. Love God, love one another, and My Father will bless you and I will come and dwell in your hearts!

I love you, My beloved ones. Strive after holiness. Just try, try to be as I have taught you. Strive after holiness, model yourself on My actions. In all things be Christ-like. Little ones, you make life hard for yourself. It is so simple: love, love, love!

May 4, 1994
Be Silent with Me

My beloved ones, I love you this day this way. I died for you. I want you to know how I am waiting for you, My most beloved ones, to come and sit with Me after Communion. Do not offend My aching Heart by leaving in such indifference and discussing the weather. You have a free will I gave to you freely. I can only beg you, but you do not listen. You want what you want. Nothing, nothing can compare to time spent with Jesus Christ, truly present in your heart after Communion.

Be with Me, stay with Me, be silent with Me. Read My letters on how I love you. I wait, I wait, I wait, I yearn, I long for you, My loved ones. Oh, please do not run! Such indifference! Sit with Me at least 20 minutes. Stay. I long for you, My beloved ones. I come to you. I enter your breast. I am God. I beg you. Your will is free. You do not hear because you do not want to hear Me, My cry coming to you. What can be more important than God in your breast? I will fill you with such gifts you will never know. Please stay with Me. Do not treat Me with such indifference. I love you so! Jesus.

We Share Union with God

R. We stand strong if we love God because we can be united when we do love Him. I have a bond with you and I love you intimately in a way that I do not love another because we share this union with God.

It is in God and only in Him that we are made one. He loves us. He gave His life for love of us. He shows us the way to love. When two people love in Him there is not division but they are closer because they are both open.

It is in loving together that we are united. I can love you even if you don't love God, but we do not have as great a bond because we are not both open to His love.

To be strong and stand against attack, we must truly love at the Center. This is the Center where God's love will reign and be our strength. We must put aside any differences with our brothers and try to settle them only in love and praying for wisdom, understanding, and counsel from the Holy Spirit to know what God wants us to know. We need God to be our loving Father, Jesus to be our loving Spouse, the Holy Spirit to love and give us His gifts, and Mary to be our most loving mother, to mother us as she mothered Jesus. What warmth in our soul! This will light the darkened night because we are filled with the love of God and we can give love.

Bathe us in Your love, God. Blessed Lady, be by our side. We are but little ones in need of direction and love. Treat us tenderly and help us to be ever grateful for all you give us. Amen.

I Was Born an Innocent Baby

R. The beginning is God-made-man, born of a virgin. He is held so lovingly in her arms. He is so perfect. She is filled with such love for Her beloved Son! The end of His life was her holding Him on her lap, His lifeless body in her arms after the world had done it's awful job on our beautiful Jesus, God-made-man!

Does this signify what this world is capable of, to take an innocent body and slaughter the baby in whatever way the world sees fit? Is this what this world is capable of? Does this world do this to our children? We are given this beautiful creation from God and look what the world does to God's creation!

But He rose to new life. He, God-made-man, was victorious. He rose and gave us new life. We, too, will rise to new life, despite the hatred of this world. Christ is victorious. The victory has been won. Death has no power over Him. Sin has no power over God. We will rise again. We will stand in glory if we stay fixed in Him. He is the victor. We are His chosen ones. It is in our commitment to follow Christ and His ways that we will be victorious. We will live forever! Alleluia. Alleluia.

In all your struggles, keep your eyes on Me, My chosen ones. Live in My love. Stay rooted in Me. You will never die. Though heaven and earth pass away, not one letter of the law will pass away. I come that you might have life and have it more abundantly, not as this world gives you life, but as I give you life. Die to the world and live in Me. I am your Savior. I come that you will live.

R.Alleluia, Alleluia. And He gave them manna from heaven and they knew His might and His light shone on each of them and they were His descendants. They were His heirs to the kingdom. Alleluia. Jesus is Lord. Alleluia.

<table><tr><td>May 6, 1994</td><td>5:00a.m.</td></tr></table>

Hold on to Me, My Child

Hold on to Me, My child. You are never abandoned by Me. I need you to do this work. Please, My sweet child, this is the persecution. You will be persecuted by those closest to you. Satan wants you stopped.

I am Jesus. I am the Son of God. I am calling you to unite with all, My child. I need you to work for Me. If you give in, He will not leave you alone.

I have chosen you for the work at hand and I need you. Let go, sweet one. I am the Alpha and the Omega.

R.I cannot see myself as "you are wrong, I am right." If I take up the sword, I will perish by the sword.

Lord, I am Your daughter. I am sinful in holding on to anger and resentment. My weapon is the burning love within my heart for Jesus, my beloved!

<table><tr><td>May 6, 1994</td></tr></table>

Be at Odds with No Man

I cannot have division. It eats at My Heart. Make amends with your brothers. Do not live with division. Live in harmony. Do not prove yourself right, them wrong. Live by the Will of the Father.

Love him who is your brother. Despite your differences, respond in love. You must do My Will, but love your brothers. Be at odds with no man. If you are doing My Will, you do not have to justify yourself.

Do it, do not explain, always love one another, no matter any differences. Division, confusion and anger are created by Satan!

Do not leave anyone without a sense of love and goodwill. It will eat at you both as the worm eats the apple. Strive for love. Pray, when you are in conflict, to act only in love. I love you and I will help you.

May 6, 1994   **4:00a.m.**
Obey Me to the Letter

My child, obey Me to the letter (the others will know they disobeyed Me). I am God. I am speaking to you. You have no hate or anger or anxiousness for any man.

I am Jesus Christ, the Son of God. I need you to do this work. You write as I dictate. You will not know what is My plan. I am God and I can change all things. I do not change a man's free will. I tell each one to obey. If he does not, then he will be held accountable.

You did as you were told. In no way does My letter conflict with My mother's messages. A decision was made to ignore My words. This displeases Me greatly! I want obedience. You did exactly as I told you and I continue to expect obedience from you. I will enkindle this. You do not fret or fume. Your job is to deliver a message.

I am Jesus and I am giving you personal love letters for My beloved children. I do not hold one letter better than another. I am Jesus. I have spoken. I have been disobeyed.

You continue to do exactly as I tell you. If they laugh or give you a hard time, you continue to obey Me exactly as I tell you. I am God and I have spoken. My ways I make clear to you. I am offended by this decision. You show no ill will. I am God and I will tend to all else. You only obey Me. Write these messages and give them to Father S____. These are messages from the Son of God. They are to be heeded. If you do not obey Me, then you are choosing on your own to disobey. One message is not better than another. My message did not conflict with My mother's messages. It was a decision that this letter of Mine should not be put out. I stated specifically that I wanted it out.

My children are hurting and they need these messages. I write so tenderly of My love! These messages will save souls. My mother's purpose is to draw men's hearts to Me. I wanted My message given out at the farm. You must obey Me. You must continue to obey Me.

Souls will suffer for not hearing the message. I want them to know of My love. You continue to do exactly as I command you to do. I ask, you can choose to obey or not obey.

I am talking here. I want to be obeyed. I want My letters to reach My beloved ones!

Where You Walk I Walk with You

I am Jesus, I am the Son of God. I come and I write to you this day for My beloved ones. Time is short. Every word I write must be heeded. The souls of your suffering brothers are at stake. Nothing matters on the face of this earth except to love God and love each other. I am the Omega, I am your all. Every moment that you live, live to draw souls to Me. Think, "How will this action lead this soul to God?"

Be so loving and pure. Nothing here matters except how you lived to love Me and one another. I am truly with you this day. In the silence you feel My presence. When you listen to the silence, feel Me with you, close and right by your side. Where you walk I walk with you. I hold your hand. I comfort you. I make all things work.

Sit you still and pray. Do not fret or fume. My hand is ever present. There is nothing that happens that I do not allow. It is in your trials that you are taught My mighty lessons.

Do not talk about your brothers and make yourself right. Live only to spread My love. If I tend to the lilies of the field, do you think I do not tend to you? I tend to every detail of your life. You answer to Me and Me alone. You fear no part of your life ever! I am tending to you minute by minute.

Oh, sweet one, not one thing matters but that you choose to know, love and serve Me. Your job is to draw others to My love. Keep forever before your eyes your brother going to heaven. In your actions, lead him to eternal life. He needs you to love in adversity. You do not worry for a thing. I watch your comings and your goings. I am forever vigilant and with you. Oh, little one, I love you so.

Treasure the moments you spend with your brother. Do not waste moments accounting events that displease you. I will tend to your every need. Do not ever show your concern and worry to your brothers. A person fixed on God is not complaining. He is still loving his brothers and silently praying for others who need prayers.

Practice holding your tongue. Satan wants you to spread a dark cloud. Spread the love of God always. In adversity spread His light to those you are with. Do not give in to rehashing events. In all things trust in Me. Give your problems to Me and know I will handle them and then be about the job of loving all.

You are so favored to have such precious children. Guard your moments with them as gems given as a gift from Me!

It is hard to put your concerns aside and trust in Me. Trust is a staircase that leads to holiness. Trust in all things and continue to be My light shining on all.

This world needs to be constantly illuminated by you. Do not give in to sadness or thoughts of making yourself right. Turn it over to Me and know I will take care of it.

Do not talk about your brothers. Control your tongue as the doorway to holiness. Trust in Me. Do not give in to any speech that does not promote love. You be at peace always. I am right by your side. You are never alone. I do not leave you for one second. I love you, My little one. Trust and let go and fall into the arms of Jesus. Be wrapped in My arms. My light surrounds you and you are My beautiful, loved ones.

Oh, how I love you!

May 7, 1994

Doing His Will

R. Doing His Will is doing His Will. He is another person. His Will is not necessarily my will, but, if I do His Will, it is how my life is in harmony with God and works out. Doing His Will causes me little problems. In the end, I have peace of mind. Maybe a struggle, maybe suffering, maybe persecution, but I have peace in that I am pleasing God.

I receive my answers in the inner promptings of my heart. Maybe I hear or see, but usually He communicates, sight unseen, inside. So why, when I am given a big command that I don't want to do, why follow it without sight, without exterior words? I follow a command, which may be so difficult, from inside, sight unseen. I do this command. This is faith, this is intimacy with Jesus, to know He truly is present. He truly communicates and I will not be at rest until I do His Will! Doing His Will is hard. It is His Will. It is not our will. It takes faith and trust in our hearts and what we are being told there. If the whole world goes one way, we must do His Will.

I love You so, my Lord. I love You for You. I can do Your Will!

God Does Not Operate as Humans Operate

R. God does not operate on your schedule. You ring, you get an answer. God's way is the way of faith. He operates in the inner promptings of your heart. He gives you His answers here.

How do you develop faith and trust when you expect God to give you answers like humans? Your faith and trust in God is what develops over time. I cannot demand that God give me an answer when I want one. Do I think I can control God too?

God does not work this way. If I do not develop faith and trust, what will I do when things are so bad? Do I think He will constantly appear and reassure me? He does not work this way with me or most of the world.

A Face of Peace Reflects A Heart of Love

How is your face, dear one? Are you anxious inside? Then your face is a reflection of your inner being. In all you do, pray to let go, pray to love. A heart that is full of love has a face that is full of peace.

Why fret and fume when I am tending to you personally? I walk by your side, sweet one. Let go and let Me do what you need done. Quit worrying. You spend your life wasting precious valuable time. Oh, sweet one, let go, let go. Please shine to the world. Let your face be the light in the dark world. Spend time alone with Me in silence. Do not think. Let My peace fill your soul. Let Me operate in your heart.

Your face, your tone of voice, your body movements, reflect the person within. If you are pulled tight inside, you will give a tight person to this world. Concentrate on showing peace in your being. Peace I leave with you, My peace I give to you, not as the world gives you peace, but real peace that warms a troubled soul.

I am your beloved Jesus. I pour My love into your heart. Come in silence and experience My peace. Let go, child. Peace be to you. I love you!

Bring Your Cares to the Foot of the Cross

I am God. I come to you to teach you a lesson. I want you to focus on Me. You feel that you are covered with cares. Put them at the foot of My cross. Tell Me all your cares and then let go. I am guarding your life. You are being followed by a band of angels. Do not fret or fume or worry about where you will go. I need you to do this work. I will guard you. You must be alone with Me. Sit in silence. Tell Me, as you are telling a friend, what is bothering you. I am God. I can do more than any human. I talk to you and you listen. Believe Me, I am truly talking here. I know exactly what you need. Come to Me when you are weary and I will give you rest.

Satan is constantly trying to tell you to worry. I am there in the unseen world and I am present to you. Focus on Me, My sweet one. I am guiding you. I am guarding you. I am by your side, child. I mean every word you hear. Listen to Me, My sweet one, I love you so!

R.God's power is so obvious. He is guiding us. We must have faith. He is truly here, guiding me. He walks by our side. I must have faith. Faith is a gift from God. Pray for faith and the strength to live by it. I must obey Him in all things to the letter. I may have a struggle, persecution, but peace that I am doing His Will, not mine.

The face reveals the person within. I preach the gospel in how I am in my being. Jesus' face is on fire for love of us. It is radiant! I could not even gaze on it, there is so much power and might! My face reflects the God within. It will radiate with His power and might if He is alive within my heart. Keep your face shining. Put aside Satan and his ways that make you bowed down. Do not wear a dark cloud about your face. Reflect the gentleness of the God within.

I am the Way, the Truth and the Life. There is no short cut, My child. I am the only way. Stay alive in My love. Trust at every moment. Trust in Me and let Me fill your heart with My peace and My love. You wait on Me, My child, and your eyes will reflect the God within. Your face is radiant as it is. Work on your interior, that which lights up your face.

Be concerned with Me. Be in love with Me. Love shines from a person's face. Be about our love affair. Be on fire for love of Me so you will radiate to your brothers. It is up to you to live in My love or choose darkness. Live in My love and radiate it to the world.

They will see the face of God within you and live. You preach the gospel in your being. Your being must be so fixed on Me! I am God. I am Love. I want to live in you and light up the darkness. Let go! I do the work. Busy yourself about our love affair. Oh, I love you. I want to have My life with you.

May 9, 1994 After Communion

Walk in the Way of the Light

R.Our feet carry us about in this world. We do not think much about our feet and how they do this job.

I have received visions of feet. In 1978, when I received a gift from God, I saw a shoe and I heard the verse, "Walk in the way of the Light."

I have a free will. My path must be the path set by the Master. He leads, I follow. His ways are not always the ways I want to follow. I sometimes do not want to forgive. I do not want to let go of hurts when I have been wronged. I want to hold on and be angry. Walk in the way of the Lord! I do not want to obey when I have a letter that is not nice, but that I must deliver. I would rather be popular and not cause any discomfort. "Walk in the way of the Lord."

Is this the same as doing His Will? I wanted to sing in the choir at the Athenaeum. I liked it. I felt important. I was singing beautiful songs to God. He took my voice away! I finally saw what His Will was for me. I wanted something very much. He didn't want me there.

I can see now so many things I wanted. I wanted to play the music at daily Mass. 'What a good thing to do!', you say? He wanted me to go to Mass and listen to His words and spend time in adoration after Mass and write these letters.

I wanted to get my children through college. I continued to teach. I lost my voice and I was miserable. I wanted to spend my time with Jesus. I spent some time with Him, but I had to work, too. I couldn't talk so I wrote up long lectures and tried to make it work. It made me miserable. For two years and two months, my voice was almost entirely out of commission but I still received special recognition for teaching. I worked hard to do a good thing. Teaching is a good thing. He was calling me to be writing these letters. I did my will and wrote some, but it was misery. I couldn't breathe because my vocal chords would swell and I had trouble breathing. Did I listen? When do we listen?

God speaks in the inner promptings of our hearts. The more I listened, the more I heard, the more I realized that I must have no preconceived ideas of what is to happen. He directs me. I knew these things were good things. I knew I was doing His Will.

I was a teacher. I went to school all those years. I had to teach. It was right. But it wasn't His Will! I can't try to think and make sense out of what is a good thing. I have to listen and wait for His answer—when He gives it. I know in my heart what He is saying, like it or not. His Will is His Will, not mine. They might be the same, or they might be entirely different, but I have to do His Will! His Will He makes clear in the inner promptings of my heart. He speaks directly to me. I must be still to hear. I have to pray every day to the Holy Spirit for His gifts. When He tells me His Will, I know it is what He wants me to do. I don't figure it out. I am told and I know I have to do it. Then He nags me until I do. To me it is like a toothache. It stops when I do His Will. It bothers me until I do it.

He told me this morning that I am not perfect. I was being pushed by my son and I got angry. Then I felt, "What is the use? I got angry. Now give it all up." He said, "You are not perfect. Say you are sorry and move on."

In my pride, I think I should be perfect and know all things and never be learning His way. His way He makes clear to us in the inner promptings of our hearts. I am human. I fall, I say I am sorry, I learn a lesson. I do not get angrier and keep on being nasty or mean and then say, "Well, this is the end of this." In humility, I say I am sorry and move on to serving our precious Lord Who loves us so. This is His way!

Walk in My way, My dear children. Walk. Your feet carry you down the road. Follow the road of the Master. If you take a bad turn, get back on the road. I am leading. I am waiting. I am walking with you where you walk. I never leave you. You move away from Me. I stay steadfastly by you.

Oh, child, be humble. Do not let pride and anger eat at your heart. When you are wrong, admit it and do My Will. I am calling you to follow Me. Follow My path. It is the only way to your happiness and peace of mind. Wherever you go, My sweet one, you never travel alone. I am with you. Love, love, love. Do not let Satan work in your head.

If I am telling you to do something, do it, even if it is unpleasant. This is what teaches you the way of the Lord. The more you obey Me, the more you hear Me. I am God. I do not necessarily communicate as you do. I may use your senses, but I do not need them to talk to you. I do not need words. I give you promptings. You know when I speak to you and you know you must follow.

Open yourselves up to Me. Pray to be open and to know how to listen to Me. I am God and I want to tell you all you need to know. No one can speak to you as I do in your heart. Come and be with

Me in silence and let Me talk to you. I love you so, dear ones. I will never steer you wrong.

R. He never told me, in the letters, to get out of the chorale. I had to hear it in my heart after much misery, as I was holding on. I went to the doctor. I took voice lessons (with no voice) for two years and two summers. I continued to take voice lessons with no voice! I took antibiotics, and could hardly breathe, but I kept teaching the next year. Did He tell me to quit? No, He waited until after I had quit and then said, "You will not have any problem with your voice if you do not teach."

He gives us promptings in our hearts. He wants us to hear with our hearts. He taught me about His ways in the letters. Things about my life I had to hear in my heart. He communicates in our hearts, directly to us. Doing His Will is doing His Will. Do we cover up what He says and do what we want? Every time I do not listen to Him I move farther from Him and I hear less because my pipeline is not clear.

I cannot disobey Him ever or I cannot stand it. If I don't do His Will, I am miserable. If the whole world hates me, I still want to do His Will.

May 10, 1994

ROSARY MEDITATIONS
The Sorrowful Mysteries

Note: These letters were received on April 25, 1994, at Medjugorje, from Our Lady.

1. The Agony in the Garden.
✠ I knew full well every blow, every wound, the crowning, the crucifixion. I saw My mother's suffering. I knew all that would happen. I sweat blood. I suffered so much mental anguish for you, beloved one, for you. I said yes to all I knew would follow, yes to you, knowing how you one day would love Me, too. Oh, how I love you. Will you say yes to the suffering I send to you? Will you say yes to loving My beloved ones? Say yes to Me today. I loved you so.

2. The Scourging at the Pillar.
♡ I am the Immaculate Heart. I love you with my tender Heart. I heard the blows they gave my Son. I could scarcely look up. I heard the blows, the awful blows. My Son stood in silence while they beat Him.

✠ All the whipping, all the brutality! The blows covered My entire body. I bled profusely. I stood in My own blood. These were My beloved ones who beat Me. They tore My flesh until it hung from My body and they laughed at their handiwork.

Do your brothers persecute you and say mean things to you? Do as I did. Respond with love. Anyone who is hating you is suffering from connectedness to Me. Pray for their conversion. Live to help them get to heaven.

3. Crowning with Thorns

✚ Think of someone you love very deeply yelling awful accusations at you. How it wounds your heart, My child. I sat there while they crowned Me with thorns and they hollered awful accusations at Me. They were My beloved ones, yet they stood there spitting at Me and hollering awful things at Me. Those whom I dearly loved, and they mocked Me and insulted Me and hurled their ugly hatred and lies at Me. I accepted all they did with a bleeding Heart and forgave them and loved them still.

Oh, you do not know suffering. Suffer for Me and lessen My load. This world is wounding My aching Heart. People are indifferent and hateful. They mistreat one another and are proud of their actions. Pray for your beloved persecutors. Don't hate them. It is as with those who tore My flesh and mocked Me. They were so engulfed in darkness! They did not know what they were doing.

All that matters is how you love Me and one another. Love those who hate you. My way is a hard way. When they hurt you and holler every ill thing at you, look to heaven and praise the Lord for the trial. It is in suffering that you are drawn closer to My precious Heart. I shed My blood for you. I suffered for you. Will you not suffer when I ask you to?

4. Carrying of the Cross

♡ I could scarcely stand to walk the way with Him. I was so sick at what they had done but I wanted to be with my Son. I walked by the grace of God.

✚ My suffering was intensified by the sorrow and suffering of My mother. My eyes met hers and I saw her red, teary face. All they did to Me, but to watch My beloved mother suffer! She heard the cross as it thumped up the hill. The sounds were so loud and, at the sight, she had to look away.

Stand by Me and walk this road to Calvary. Listen and see My beaten body. Hear the jeers of the crowd. Hear the thumping of the cross. Listen when it falls hard on Me and I can scarcely go any more. Walk with Me and be there, then think of the little crosses I

ask you to carry. Do not put them down. Accept them for Me. It is
in your crosses that you are drawn closer to Me. I endured all this
suffering for deep and ardent love of you and I would do it today
for you alone.

5. The Crucifixion

♥ They hung Him on the cross. I was so weak I could barely stand.
I was held up by John. I watched my Son in such agony. Oh, my
beloved Son! What had He done to deserve such suffering? He
loved you to His death. He was crucified for love.

✠ How do I tell you that I died for you? Do you even know I would
do it today, just for you? They nailed My beautiful hands and feet to
the cross. Big, gigantic nails they pounded into My precious hands.
Such hard hearts! They pounded the nails through My feet. Blood
spurted out and they continued. Such hardness of hearts. Look at
your hands, My child. Would you allow someone to nail them to a
cross? Would you withstand this torture for love? This is My love
for you. It is not a little lip service love. It is the love that made Me
lay down My life for you.

Surrender. I call you to surrender. Open your arms as I did when
I died on the cross. Let all your worldly possessions drop around
you and you will experience the joy of being free, united only to
Me, of letting go and knowing that I, God, tend to your every need.
To My death on the cross I loved you and I love you this way this
very day. Let go and give it all to Me. I will care for you far better
than you could for yourself. I am God and I love you more than you
can love yourself.

R.Jesus is dead, hanging on the cross, arms outstretched. His feet
are not even on the ground. He is hanging by nails on a piece of
wood. What do we hold on to? He wants us in midair in total
surrender.

Oh, little ones, how you squander your possessions. How you
hold on to people, how you won't let go! See Me in total surrender. I
gave My very life for you. What do you hold on to, My little ones?
Little bits and pieces you give to Me and you hold tightly to your
lives. All will go up in smoke and only the things of God will
remain. Not one pair of shoes do you take with you, only your love
given to God and to others.

Suffer for Me

Do not put the cross down. Do not complain. Sainthood is carrying the cross with a cheerful face. Your brothers will not comfort you and they will not give you your answers. Turn to Me, My beloved ones, in the silence. I am forever present. I know the workings of your hearts. I sanctify your souls. I am the Sacred Heart of Jesus. I ponder your ways with such love.

When you suffer, do not think you are alone. I am closest when you suffer. Turn to Me. I walk with you. You carry My cross with Me. Oh, how My Heart aches in your ailing brothers. They do not even know their ways. They curse one another and hate. They have lost all sense of God. Where will they see his love if you turn your back to Me? I need you to love. It is persecution to live in this world. Your brothers are in darkness. You are the light that shines in their dark souls. You can't put your cross down. You can't complain and feel downhearted. Satan is so glad when you are bowed down. You must trust in Me and My ways at every moment. Everything you experience I allow. Do not fight it. If Satan is bothering you, cast him out, but accept the crosses I send you.

Meditate on My Passion. I accepted My suffering. I was silent. I did not argue and try to prove Myself right. Peace is found in knowing God will take care of you. You may be suffering but He is allowing it. Accept it with great joy. Suffering is partaking in My life. My life was given for you. The way to Me is the way of the cross. Don't throw these powerful graces back in My face. Practice silence. Do not complain to your brothers. Come and complain to Me. If others notice your silence, pray to say only what is loving and what will draw them to God.

Your job, 24 hours a day, is to love and lead others to heaven. Nothing else matters. If you stop and judge yourself by the world's standards, you will be confused. Keep your eyes on Me.

Do not look at your brother and judge your actions by his. Judge your actions by My actions. I am the Master. I show you the way. I lead you down the path to everlasting life.

Let go, sweet one. I will hold you up when you are down. My suffering is a gift I give you. Don't complain. Say thank you. You will be strengthened and grow in your love of Me if you accept all I send you in peace.

I know exactly what you need. I ask you to suffer. I ask you not to ask why or give it back. I ask you to accept it and love it and love your brothers. This is My way. This is the only way. Where do you run from the Lord? If you go to the heavens, I am there. Wherever you go, I am there. You cannot run from Me.

You are the light that shines in the dark night. You are a candle set on a hill that shines to those who pass by. Let My light shine from you.

I Ask You to Obey

Put your trust in Me. I do not ask you to analyze what I am doing. I ask you to obey. I truly will take care of you. If the whole world goes one way, you do as you are told. I want obedience even when you do not want to do what I am asking you to.

I ask for a clean heart. I ask you to act as I have acted. This is hard in this world. The world tells you to stand up for yourself and be aggressive. I tell you to love your brothers and be kind to them, to love your brothers as yourselves, to be willing to die for your brothers. This takes submission. It takes letting your ego go and yielding to love. It hurts sometimes to let go of self and love your brother. This is My way. They tore My flesh and I forgave them. Like an innocent lamb led to the slaughter, I was crucified. Did I fight back and justify Myself? Live to love. When others are haughty and mean, you think of Me, Jesus Christ, the Son of God and how I love you. Then forgive them and let go.

The way you act when you model yourself after Me is not the way the world acts. Do not be attached to this world. Be attached to Me. Your purpose is to love. No one has any power over you. They may persecute you but I am guarding you in your suffering. Suffer with Me. Be a fool for Christ. Love for Me. This world needs the love of Christ. If you respond as the world does, I cannot love through you.

Your will is entirely free. I call you to model yourself after Me. I in no way took up the sword! My way is love! I cannot love your brothers through you if you choose to follow the world. The way of the world is the self. My way is selflessness. This takes submission of your self and yielding to a higher cause.

Rita, this is the way to peace in your heart. When you do My Will, even when you do not want to, you have peace. You will not have peace until you deliver the letter I told you to. You must obey Me, child, in every detail. You do not know My mind and My ways and it is not up to you to analyze them. I want obedience from you. You are making things harder by stalling. You, My sweet one, will be tested in fire. You will be molded in My special oven. I will melt you in the oven of My Heart. Come and enter there and put all your trust in Me.

Remember the furnace of My Heart. Come to Me. It is hot with the fire of My love, but it is your refuge. You enter there, you are changed into My special soldier of love. Nothing to fear for it is a vat of love. You jump in where others fear to tread. I am the Sacred Heart of Jesus. He who enters My Heart will be refreshed and molded by My love. Nowhere else will you find such love and peace!

Oh, child, I love you. Please do not tarry. Trust the God Who loves you and talks to you daily. How will others trust and have faith if you do not have it yourself? You preach the gospel in your being. When you surrender to Me, you will be free.

You are running your life. Let go, child. You will feel a surge, as if someone lifted a load. Let go to Me. I will not lead you astray. You are holding on when you need to let go. Do not test Me. I know every little thought you have. You cannot fool Me. I know your heart better than you.

Tell Me your faults and ask for help. Don't hide any. I am there to help you. If you do not admit them yourself, you cannot improve. I know every way you need to improve far better than you. Come to Me. Come into My Heart. Be free in My love. This is the way, the only way to peace of mind.

If you go to the heavens, I am there. You, child, can never run from Me. I ardently love you. Surrender and be free.

May 11, 1994 After Communion

Fast for Me

If you seek any gratification in this world, it is only momentary. Nothing that you seek here will be an end in itself. You fool yourself. You think you aren't attached. Then it is taken away and you start to kick and scream. "Why, God? Why this?" You are so attached to people and jobs and food and you do not know how attached you are until you are forced to give it up. Fasting is a way to teach you to give up your attachments. Fasting is a way to discipline yourself. Fasting is a way to holiness. If you constantly reward yourself with food, you are attached to food. I call you to holiness. Holiness is not easy. Fasting is not easy. You must eat properly, eat good bread that will sustain you often through the day. Drink a lot of water. You will feel better than if you ate food. I am in control. Go to Communion as often as possible. Communion is the true Body of Jesus Christ.

The way to Me is surrender. The way to Me is doing as I will you to do. Your union with Me depends on your doing the Will of the Father, surrendering yourself, giving in when you don't want to, loving when you don't want to. Pray to love as I will you to love. You do not even know how far you are from holiness. Pray to be holy. Pray for surrender. Pray to be selfless. Pray My Prayer for Union with Me. If you are gratifying yourself with worldly things, you are keeping yourself from Me. This world is passing. I need your sacrifices. Souls are at stake. You can help save a soul from eternal damnation through your prayers and sacrifices. Do you realize this? Live to draw others closer to Me and to help souls to get to heaven. Play the song, "Thank You for Giving to the Lord."

My way is not easy. You are not gratified here in worldly things. You go so far, then the devil says, "Don't fast." Fast this day. You can help to save souls from the fires of hell by your prayers today. You can lead others back to Me with your sacrifices. Do you want your brothers to be converted? Then fast! Mortify yourself. Eat good food on the other days. Constantly sacrifice. Sustain yourself with food. Do not live to gratify yourself with food!

I am calling you to holiness and sainthood. Do you want to convert your brothers? Then do as I ask. The devil will try to get you to eat and tell you that you needn't fast. I want you to fast this day. You will be okay health-wise. I am God. The hairs of your head are numbered, child. I have all the power! Pray for your beloved brothers. Time is so short. You can help your brothers on their journey for eternal life. Will you answer My call? Fast for conversions. Please, I beg you this day, say "yes" to Me!

May 11, 1994

The Eucharist Is Your Miracle!

I handle each soul individually. I give you exactly what you need to do My work. It is in acceptance of what I give you that you will learn what you need to learn. Here is your will again. You want your way. I do things My way. I am God. I know all things. Surrender, child. Do as I ask you to do. If I wanted to give you visions and signs, I would. I give you as I know you will need.

You must teach others to find Me in their hearts. I am as present as I am when you see Me. If you see Me, you believe. Blessed is he who does not see and believes!

I am giving you what you need. Quit trying to look for signs and wonders. My children, My children, I am present in your hearts! I, Jesus Christ, the Son of God, come to you in Holy Communion. I come inside of you. Do you see the miracle in this?

Spend time with Me after Communion. Don't look anywhere else. I, Jesus, am truly there and you walk away from Me and do senseless things. Then you want a sign? A sign is not as powerful as God within your breast! You miss the magnificence of this gift, child. God, truly present, dwells within you after Holy Communion. Be with Me. Listen in the silence. I will talk to you in your heart.

The risen Christ is with you at every Mass and enters your body. This is a miracle. Do you realize how present I am to you? This is the miracle I give to you. If I appeared to you, I am not closer than this. Relish the gifts I have given you. You want more? You weaken your relationship with Me. I communicate in your hearts. I need you to preach that God is truly talking in the inner promptings of your heart. Who will preach this if you yourself do not know. Come sit in silence with Me. Be still one hour a day. It is so little when I give you 24 hours. No one has the answers you need. No one on this earth knows what you need to know. Quit asking humans supernatural questions. Come to Me and I will give you all you need.

May 12, 1994   6:00a.m.

Faith Is the Answer

My precious child, did I not say you would be persecuted by those closest to you? Dear one, I am ever by your side. If the earth is shaken and the stars do not give their light, I will be by your side.

It is in the silence that you feel My presence. I am truly present to you now in this struggle. Blessed are they who have not seen and have believed. You must teach others to know Me in their hearts. My answers I give to you in the silence. My presence can be felt in the silence. I am truly here, dear one.

Faith is the answer. Faith will see you through. I do not come and ring bells and tell you what you need to know. There is a oneness in your heart. Your answers are found within. Teach all how to communicate with Me. I am truly there. I am talking to you and you did as I told you to do. Have peace, little one. All that matters is the life hereafter. Signs and symbols will not give you faith. You must come and be with Me. Spend time alone with Me. I wait for you in the tabernacle.

My beloved one, let go and be at peace. Though the earth be shaken, it is your faith within that will sustain you. I call you to holiness. I call you to surrender. I call you to a life of sainthood. There is peace in distress if you are fixed in Me. No weeds can live in a well cared for garden. Weed out any flaws in your lives, My children. I ponder your hearts. There is not one thing hidden from My eyes. Purity of heart in all things. Unless you achieve this purity, you shall not have union with Me as I desire

R.Create in me, oh, Lord, a clean heart, that I may more worthily serve You and worship You as the true God of all ages. Any offense is a big offense to unity with You. Oh, Lord, that I could see as You see my soul. I long for You with all my heart. My heart thirsts for Your love. You are my God, my all. From You flow the waters of everlasting life. Alleluia.

May 12, 1994

Your Love Is What I Crave

R.I sought and I searched. I tried to find relief from the pain. I loved through my kids and wanted their love back. I tried to be loved by someone, and no one was ever there. Oh, Lord, in desperation I came to You and cried at Your feet. You sat so patiently with me. You loved me each time I came and I found peace, peace and love that no one else had!

When I left You, I cried because no one gave to me as You did. Now, Lord, I know no one can give me what I crave, my soul craves You! I long for Your love. You are so gentle, so loving, so kind, so full and always there, Lord, no matter how I am upset, happy, whatever. You love me just the same. Who am I to know this love!

Jesus, Jesus, my Lord, my God, my all, how can I love You as I ought?

Love for Me, My child. This is how you love Me: what you do to the least of your brothers you do to Me. Walk in My ways. When they persecute you and holler at you, love them, love them, love them. You are learning about love, child. Do not give way to anger and hate and guard your tongue always. This is the way you receive Me. Guard that spot, make it holy, do not cast stones at your brothers. Always love them.

R.My God, I seek You. My soul thirsts for You. Your love is finer than life.

May 12, 1994 After Communion	8:45a.m.

Your Tongue Is the Doorway to Holiness

Let you who are without sin cast the first stone. Control your tongue as the doorway to your soul. Your tongue is the doorway to holiness. I am Jesus. I am the Son of God. Harken to My words here for I speak and I speak clearly to you, My precious children. Satan will work in your minds to create hatred. He aims to destroy you and your peace of mind. You must come and be with Me, so close, after Communion. Be silent with Me. Let Me pour out My peace to you!

Guard your tongues. Guard your hearts. Guard your minds. You must think you are holy. Satan aims to trip you up. He uses your weakest link. He works in your minds to create dissension. I am speaking in your hearts. Come and be with Me. I fill you. You need to be in constant connectedness with Me. Love is the answer. You cannot love Me and hate your brother. I love your brother. I shed My life for him whom you hate. Your Father created him. His special creation! Open your hearts. Lay away your pride and your egos, focus on your goal to love God and draw your brothers to eternal life. You cannot do this alone. Satan is an evil force that aims to stop you. You are in a daily battle, little ones. Are you worn out at the end of the day? Fight the good fight. Your arms are your love of God and love for one another. You cannot love and hate at the same time.

Open up your hearts to My love. You need to be alone with Me. You need My supplies. You must constantly choose to love and not be angered at your brothers. Satan is pressing down on you who aim to spread My work. He works on the priests and sisters. He works in marriages. He works on children to annoy their parents. He works in your hearts and talks through your tongues. Be aware how strongly he is pressing on you, My faithful ones.

You must constantly silence him and choose to love your brother. He is not perfect and neither are you. It is your love that will bind you together. There is no room in your heart for hate. Hate and love cannot co-exist. A heart must be pure to love. Let go of all your anxieties. You have to come to Me. You cannot fight this battle alone.

No matter what your brother does, pray for him and love him and come to Me for your guidance. Do not talk about each other and make yourself right and them wrong. Pray and sacrifice. Satan is getting a strong hold on My faithful ones through anger in their hearts. Do not give in to pride and anger. Only love will do. Love one another as I have loved you.

Let go of your foolish anger and resentments. Love one another. I love you and I am present to you this very day. What more do you need when God loves you so much?

Forgive your brothers when you feel wronged. Pray to let go of your anger at one another. Pray to forgive. Do not talk about your brothers. Love them. Only in unity will you light the city. Love will flow from your hearts and My might will abound in your souls. I love you so!

R. I do not need to talk about anyone. Tell Jesus. He listens, He knows, He has all the answers! I do not need to tell anyone anything derogatory about anyone else. When I am making myself right and others wrong, I am missing a chance to spread God's love.

God is truly there and He will tend to all my cares. I must trust and love and have faith in Him. Amen. It doesn't matter what the world thinks if I focus on the immensity of His love.

It is in this struggle that you realize the immensity of My love. Feel the flutter in your chest, the burning of My love deep within. I am here, little one, I am here. It is this struggle that I have given you this moment. You grow in your trials and our love is deepened. Your time is My time.

Do as I ask. Spread My love!

May 15, 1994
Love Your Children

Dear child, do not worry for I am ever beside you. I walk with you wherever you go. This life is but a passing moment, here today, gone tomorrow. Let go and surrender into My hands. I have work for you to do. Do it and let Me run the show.

What love you gave is all that lives. It lives in the hearts of all you touch. It is your kindness that is not forgotten.

It is your love that ripples to your children and brothers. Such needless tasks you perform, and deem so very important, and your children are left tended to by a sick television. You are responsible for your children.

I have given you them to be loved and directed. All your foolish endeavors, and the children are ignored. You are going nowhere fast. Do you want to race down a road that leads to a dead end? What a frustrating experience, to hurry, hurry, and then a dead end! How many of your jobs are really a race to a dead end?

How many of your jobs are willful jobs that you want accomplished but really serve no purpose? Did you set the goal and decide that you would do it and now you are going to carry it out to prove to yourself you need to do as you intended? Is it a useless task? What about your children? What about your role as a mother or father or spouse? How many goals do you plan that are totally useless, but you carry out as a law that should not be broken, while your family is ignored?

How you love God and love one another is all that matters. Useless tasks are soon washed up from the sea and laid lifeless on the beach. The life in your actions is how you treat each other. Love is life and it doesn't die. It is given and is acted out in the actions of others. Is it so hard to love or are you just performing needless tasks and are not in the habit of giving love?

Love lives forever. Love is never forgotten. Love given to your children is still given years later.Love is planted in the hearts as life! Love your children always. Love planted in children is a treasure. They are young and it remains so much longer. They will meet so many more people. America, love your children! They are thirsty for your love. They are given a cold world. They are given things and games and television and dreams and education and money. What happened to time in prayer? What happened, America, to love in their hearts?

Give the children the gift of God's love within you. Your answer, America, is in praying and playing with your children, not competitive sports to make you better, then not so good, but games to promote good, healthy feelings of friendship and love. Walk with your children. Tell them about God. Show them kindness. Show them peace. Give them time. How will you teach your children to have peace when you have none yourself?

You don't have time for them? What a seed to plant in their little hearts. Take time! Giving time develops their self esteem. Not having time robs them of their importance. Children need you. They need your love. They need your time. They need you to pray with them. If God gave you a child, it is His Will that you are a parent. Being a parent is a job.

I ask you, My beautiful parents, to take your job seriously. This is the most important job you have, being a parent! It is not second to what you think is important. You are giving life to a child. This life lasts forever. To teach them they are not worth your time is a sick lesson. I want you to love and spend time with My beloved little ones. Forget your crafts and picture shows, your games, all the little jobs you assign yourselves that must get done. You will be held accountable to God for how you raised your children. You are responsible for teaching your children about God.

My time is given to you to do My work. It is not your time at all. You have a free will. God will hold you accountable for how you spent your time. Time is a valuable asset. To squander it for yourself is wrong. God created you to know, love and serve Him. Are you using your life to do His Will?

Go to Jesus—He Loves You

R. He sits in the tabernacle and He hears all that goes on about Him. He longs for you to come and spend time in adoration and love. He is God, truly God, and He awaits you with such love.

Churches are full. How is your heart to behold the Son of God? Are you anxious to be here? This is God, child. Are you ready to be in His house?

He sits here in the tabernacle with such love to give. Do you genuflect when you walk in front of the tabernacle. Do you realize that the same Jesus Who died and gave His life for you is there? Oh, how He waits for you to come. He waits with such eagerness for you to come and tell Him you love Him.

He wants you to know He is in Communion. He loves you so. He comes to you inside of your body. He loves you so. He gave the priest the power, through the Holy Spirit, to change bread and wine into His Body and Blood so He could be present to you, Body and Blood, Soul and Divinity, in the Eucharist. Nothing you ever do here on earth can compare to receiving God inside of your heart. He is a real Person. He is with you this day, the same Jesus Who died on the cross.

He loves you so much! He would die this very day just for you alone. Think of a friend that would die for you. It is hard to share part of our delicious cake with a friend. He gave His life for you because He loved you so much.

He asks only two things of us: to love God and love one another. He wants us to love each other so much that we would give our all for each other. When someone is hurting and being mean, he needs our love more. He doesn't need us to be mean to him.

God is asking you to love your friends today. When they are mean, don't argue with them. See the creation of God the Father in them and pray for them. Your prayers and sacrifices can stop wars. Pray the rosary. It is so powerful!

Remember always: God truly loves you! When you feel unloved, go to Jesus. He is always waiting for you with love. Mary is your mother. She mothers you the same as she mothered Jesus. Pray to her.

Help Me, Lord, to Do As I Ought

You, My child, are guarded by My hand when you learn to let go and do as I ask. You must realize I am forever with you and you do not need to worry. Trust in Me, trust in Me, trust in Me! I am Jesus Christ. I am the Son of God. Do not worry or fume or fret. Be ever attentive to My presence with you. Let go, sweet one, and let Me get close to you.

Satan is tormenting you. Pray for trust and give it all up. I love you with such love. Do not worry ever. I am by your side in your darkest hours. Trust, child. You are so far from trusting Me!

R. When people are hurting, say you are sorry. It is not as if you made them hurt, but it helps them to know someone is sorry. They are suffering, they need your compassion and love. I wondered why Jesus kept telling me to say I was sorry when they were mad. They need to know you are sorry that they are suffering, that they are feeling hurt. To say you are sorry will help their hurting hearts. It is in love and compassion that we should respond to one another. To say we are sorry is to suffer with our beloved brothers.

Be loving in all things. Choose love. Do not seek yourself. Come and let Me heal your aching heart and be loving to My hurting ones. I love them so. Show them compassion and care. Do not be hard on your brother when he wrongs you. See the suffering heart inside of him and love him. Love is the answer! Be compassionate to one another. This is how you put on Christ. Be Me to your hurting brothers. They need you to love Me. If you love Me, you will love one another. All works out when you love God and love each other. You do not love and then you wonder why the problem. The problem is your lack of love for one another. Give love to each other. I cannot say this enough. It is in loving that your heart will find peace. Surrender to love. It is healing. I am the Way, the Truth and the Life. My ways I make known to you in the recesses of your heart. Hear My gentle voice as I tell you to love. Forgive your brothers and love them.

Alleluia. This is the key to your life. Life you will have when you love each other.

You Were Hungry and I Sent Manna from Heaven

I am Jesus Christ, the Son of God. Come to Me. I love you. Be not fixed to the things of this world. Harken to Me, My child. I am truly here. I died that you might live. Tell them and be attentive to Me, for you were hungry and I fed you. I gave you manna from heaven and you knew I truly was present and in your midst. Harken to Me. I call out to you and come with such longing for your love. I wait. I wait. Why do you worry for such useless tasks? Oh, child, God is truly here, but you go after such senseless things. When will you hear? Will you remain deaf forever? Listen, give Me your love, sweet one. I beg you to be attentive to Me. My Heart is aching to love you more. I cry out to you and you do not hear. I am the Alpha. I am the Omega.

Come for My ardent love, child. I cry out to you. Take the time and harken to My pleading. I give you all you need. Why do you go to other places? Oh, I love you, I love you, I love you. I am the Sacred Heart of Jesus, burning and on fire for love of you. I am here. I love you so.

R.There is such burning in my chest to behold You, Jesus Christ, the Son of God. The world stands still and in the moment I catch a glimpse of eternity.

I am your God and you know the glories of heaven. What you feel is only a drop in the sea. What glories await him who loves and serves the Lord. Your delights will be beyond any comprehension for I am truly God and I declare it so this very day. You will be with Me forever in heaven! Live to love and serve Me! Do not waste one precious moment in remorse. Live only to draw others to everlasting life. Your job is so important! Souls are at stake. Souls are being lost. You hold the mighty medicine to turn hearts to the ardent on-fire love of Jesus and I say to you, "Come, My beloved ones, creations of My dear Father, worry not for yourselves, but harken to My call to love God and your brothers." It is in the realization of this calling, through Me, that you will help others to be led to heaven.

I am the Way, the Truth, the Life. I lead, you follow. You love and your hearts will radiate Me from inside of you. I want to live from your being. I want to be one in you. I want to operate and reach My beloved ones through you. Harken to My call. Please do not say, "No, I am too busy". Nothing here matters if it is not My work.

Come to Me and be fed by Me Who loved you to My death and

beckons you to answer My call. Live in My love and live to love God and your brothers. Nothing else matters, My child.

I am the Sacred Heart of Jesus. I am on fire, on fire, on fire for love of you! You get up, you walk away and God awaits you, My precious children. I am offended so by your indifference. Come and let Me caress you. Let Me hold you. Let Me feed you. I am God, little ones, do you hear Me?

R. Time stands still and I behold my Lord. His kingdom is not of this world. I behold the Son of God, truly present and in our midst. In the silence we will know His presence. He is truly alive and here with me this day. The closer I get to Him, I become one in Him and He becomes one in me. Oh, such oneness, to be united to God this way! Is anything of any more importance than being one in God? Jesus, make me one in You and let me know Your Father, my Father, through this union with You.

Oh, blessed of My Father, to experience the love of the one, triune God, Father, Son and Holy Spirit!

R. How are we so blessed with this love and the love of Mary, our mother? My heart pants for this love of God. That man can achieve such union with God, that we can be one in Him and He one in us is so unbelievable. This is how we share our love with one another. There is a oneness when we ardently love Jesus. We are close to others because of His love in us. The more we love God, the more we can love each other. There is an openness that we have that allows us to love as He loves through us.

I will become one in you. You will become one in Me as you open your hearts to My love. Be open, little ones. I want to love you and love through you. Empty yourself of any impurities in your heart. Forgive your brothers. Do not be angry. Keep yourselves clean and free from sin. Go to Confession. Fast, My beloved ones. It is in fasting you are drawn close to Me. Do not give in to yourselves. Discipline yourselves. This will increase your union with Me.

I am God. There is no better reward for your efforts than to achieve union with God. I want this union with you. It is you who keep us apart. Die to yourself, child, and live in Me. You must surrender your lives to Me and let Me operate your very being. Die to self and live in Me.

R. Alleluia. And they knew new life. It was the life of Christ that dwelled within them. Praise the Lord! Praise and honor to the one, true God, Father, Son and Holy Spirit.

He constantly says, "Unite in My love. I call you to be one in Me. I am sent from the Father that you shall be one in Us."

I am He Whose bootstraps you are unworthy to tie, yet I come with such love for you. You will be one in Us. Unite in My love. Go out into the world, spread the gospel, go to the highways and the byways, spread My love. My love is the way. You will unite and become one when you love in Me for there is no division in a heart of God. You must be one in Us. As the Father has sent Me, I send you into the world to spread My love. Will you answer My call? Harken, for time is short. Your brothers are in need of this work. In your actions of love you will preach My gospel. Go and love one another as I have loved you.

R. Unity and love are coexistent. Hate and love do not coexist. I must love, love everyone. He died for my precious brother. I must love more and more like Him.

He is talking about unity. Unity is only achieved through loving. To hate any man causes division. My heart must be pure, free from all hate. I cannot do this alone. I need God's love to love my brothers as He is calling me to do.

May 18, 1994   3:00a.m.
There Is Power in Prayer

My dear one, come and be counted by the hand of God. You must work swiftly, for time, child, is short. Every moment must be spent in drawing your fellowman to God. Pray constantly. No one realizes the real power of prayer. Pray the rosary, pray with your children, pray the Holy Spirit prayers, pray, pray, pray!

And I say unto you, "Heaven and earth may pass away, but not one letter of My law will ever pass away." Do not doubt. You do not have time for such nonsense! You know exactly your mission. Do it. Satan will constantly work on you. Forget him and pray. Your job is quite evident.

You need to lead souls to My most Sacred Heart. I am the Alpha and Omega. I am your all. I do all the work and you, child, are working for Me. No one can stop it but you. Ask for grace to believe, faith to know. Ask and you shall receive. Seek and you shall find. Knock and it will be opened unto you.

R. Alleluia. Alleluia. And He made them fishers of men!

You are a fisher among men. Believe. Pray for faith, child. Yours is as shaky as some who need to see everything. After all I write to you! How you spend your mind in deliberation. Stop it! Stop it!

Trust in Me, My beloved ones. This is for real. Read the Blue Book. Get your answers. Think of My presence with you all day and night. Quit analyzing your data for a conclusion. Believe, pray one solid hour, uninterrupted, in front of Me in the tabernacle! I love you. Amen. Amen. Do you not believe I will care for you? You doubters, let go and see Me before you, clothed in white. See My mother by My side. We walk the barren earth with you and you are raised up to such heights.

I come to you, My sweet one, in the night. Do not cast Me off. Be attentive to My pleading. Tell all of My Real Presence in the Eucharist. Jesus is in your midst this day. He loves you so.

May 19, 1994 After Communion at Father Smith's Chapel
We Are United in Communion

I am one in you and you are one in Me. As the Father has sent Me, you are one in Us. I am in your body, child, at this moment. I am inside of you. I love you with such intensity. No union is greater than the union you experience after Communion. I am united to you after Communion. Pray for openness to grow in your relationship with Me. Now is the time to throw yourself into My arms and be totally open.

I am your precious Jesus, your Savior. I am God. I am present inside of your breast. Focus on Me and Me alone. Focus on Me before you receive Me. You must let go of your attachments to worldly concerns and thoughts. Drive them from your mind. They keep you from union with Me.

I am your all. I am present and by your side always. Do not belabor points in your head. I care for you as a mother cares for her baby. Babies do not plan and worry. Let go and surrender to Me. I am hyper-vigilant and by your side.

Oh, child, I love you so. I tend to your every need. Be with Me now. Let go. Surrender and be totally alone with Me. Free yourself in your mind of any attachments. Focus only on Me. I am one in you and you are one in Me. At this moment, be totally in My arms. Oh, how I love you, My beautiful one.

May 19, 1994
The Way to Him Is the Way of the Cross

R. He went out in such pain. Why should I be free? Suffering and pain teach us to let go. When I am experiencing intense pain, I cannot experience it without letting go. It is in suffering that I am drawn closer to Jesus. If I let go, I jump into His waiting arms. Intense pain...let go...forced to...Faith and trust...let go...Hairs of our head are numbered...don't have time to fume and fret and focus on self...constant letting go, giving to Him and trusting...I sit still...others move around me and bump their heads...He walks up and gives us what we need...The more I do it, the more I botch it up!

My Peace I Give You

R. Dear Jesus, let me be alone with You and in Your presence.

I am the Way. I am the Truth. I am the Life. I am the Sacred Heart of Jesus. Be at peace, My child. I truly write to you. Block out all distractions and worries of who is watching. Do not care. I am God and I speak to you here. Let go. Totally let go and put yourself in My presence. I am the Son of God. I have chosen you to write this message for My world. Pay no heed to anything or anyone around you. You are in a smoke screen. You are alone with Me.

My peace I give to you. Be at peace. Wash yourself totally clean. Where there is anger or resentment, anxiety or doubt, wash it away by the springs of living water. I wash your cares out and fill you with a warm spring of flowing grace. It transcends from My Father into your soul. You are bathed by the love of God. The Spirit fills you with His life and you are made whole, child, by the presence of the one, triune God.

My mother is constantly with you. You are in a state of total peace and acceptance, acceptance to all that is sent your way. Live the moment in surrender and know every second is allowed by My loving hand. Do not be anxious for I go with you on your way. You do not trod alone. You do not ever need to feel abandoned for I am by your side.

Little one, little one, how do I tell you these things? How do I tell you I write to you and you must harken to My call to you to listen? I will not make you respond. You have a free will. Read every letter with the conviction I, Jesus, the Son of God, speak directly to you. I profess ardently every day My love for you and you do not listen. How this hurts Me! How do I shake you? I am present and speaking here, child. Listen to Me now and be attentive to My call to summon you to complete surrender to the Will of God. I will you to stay connected to Me and My Heart. Put yourself inside of My Heart and dwell there in perfect peace. I wrap you in the fire of My love for you and all fear, doubt and anxiety are dismissed. Only I, God, can give you as you need. Let go. Let go. Let go. You are uptight and holding on to such petty things when I am speaking here to you.

I bathe you in a bath of love. I fill you. You are transcended beyond the heights of any man to the realm of the spirit and He, the Spirit, embraces you and fills you with His life and love.

Love My beloved ones. Cast out Satan. Oh, dear one, how he wants your heart. He wants to snuff out the life in you. Live in Me. Surrender to the life of God—one, true, triune God—Father, Son and Holy Spirit. Surrender to Our love. Feel the love of your mother. She mothers you as she mothered Me. Let it all go and be wrapped in Our arms. Amen. Let go, child. I cannot tell you more plainly. Pray for faith. Pray for the gifts of the Spirit. Where you were once blind, you now see.

Pray to see as I wish you to see. Open up your heart to Me. Open and remain open. When you are among your brothers, let My spirit and love flow through you to others. Pray the Prayer for Union with Me. You are My empty vessel. Oh, little one, open wide your gates. Open your eyes. You will see the world as I want you to. Open to the eyes of God. You are My beloved. Let Me operate you and do My work through you. Be so selfless that you let yourself go and let Me operate from you. I am Jesus, Son of God. I love you, My beloved. Let go and open yourself to all I have planned for you. You I call this day to do My work. You must become putty in the hands of the potter. Be selfless and live in My love.

May 21, 1994
Do Not Be Troubled or Afraid

My dear child, I love you. Constantly focus on Me and My love for you. I am Jesus, Son of the Living God. I live in the hearts and souls of My beloved ones. I have life in this world in you. The more you read these letters, the more I live in you.

I come, you write. Do not be troubled or afraid. Your love for Me and your brothers is all that matters. You think I am not right by your side. I am, child. Come and be close to Me. I want to share Myself with you.

Time is short and you will be tested. Stand still and do not give in to your emotions. Focus on Me and My love for you. You are My soldier in this cold world. I come and comfort you. Do not be troubled and anxious. Only live in My love, My sweet one. Do not worry for I am your beloved one. I love you. Jesus.

Pray the Prayer for Union with Me

Now you come to Me, after you struggle! Come to Me first, sweet one. You let Satan work in you. Satan is division. His whole work is to divide you. Know that he is forever about. You are in a daily war. Pray to be strong. You cannot do it alone.

I am Jesus Christ, the son of God. I come to give you life. I am He Who loves you ardently, My little, sweet, faithful ones. I never leave your side. I am there from your birth, right by your side, waiting to be close to you. You push Me aside and try to do it yourselves. Surrender, My beloved ones, to Him Who loved you to His death. I will sustain you and give you all you need.

Pray My Prayer For Union with Me. I want to be one with you. Come and pray with Me after Communion and in front of the tabernacle. My gift I give to you is Myself. I come to you, Body and Blood, Soul and Divinity, in Communion. I want so much to share such love with you. I long for our union. Will you harken to busy yourself about our union? Everything in your life will work out if you spend one hour with Me in adoration. I give you all you need.

My beloved ones, here today, gone tomorrow and all you hold on to is up in smoke. I am your beloved Savior. I come to you with such love. Be open and let yourself go. Experience My ardent, on-fire love. I have all the power. I can do all things. Pray the Prayer for Union with Me. Be silent with Me. It is in the silence you can experience My presence so deeply. Come and be silent with Me. Let Me work in your heart. Your time is not your time. I loan it to you to do My work. Do not be rushed and worry for what you are to do. Give it to Me and watch your work fly. I can do all things. Your job is to love God and love one another. Be not attached to your work and the job at hand. Surrender and let Me accomplish My work through you.

I need you to live your life for Me. This is your job, to love God and love one another and to draw others to get to heaven. Preach the gospel this day in your being. When the road is rocky, turn it over to Me. I am there, little one. You hold on to such useless things! None of this matters. Your focus is to serve Me!

I love you with such an ardent love. My love is the same love that led Me to My death. I will never abandon you. I loved you to My death. I wait for you. I long for you. I want to share My immense love with you this day. When you receive the love of God, you will have the strength to give love to those who are hurting. You cannot do it alone. You are in a battle and your arms are your hearts filled with My love.

Give, give, give. And, when you are weary, see My suffering face on the way to Calvary. I did not fight, I did not answer back. I accepted with love My cross and I gave My love to you. Oh, beloved, study My Passion. It is in this study you realize how much I truly loved you. You may know a little of how I love you, but you cannot fully comprehend My love. I love you, I love you, I love you. I am Jesus, Son of the Living God. Come to Me, My little ones, I love you ardently.

Pray. Prayer can end wars. Hold the crucifix.

May 22, 1994 At Medjugorje Conference	11:30a.m.

Give Me, Lord, Your Love and Your Grace

R. How do You see me, Lord? How is my soul? Work in me, God. Open me, Spirit, to Your wisdom. I am Your servant.

Let me live to please You in all my thoughts and actions, in every desire. Let it come from love of You. Oh, how I indeed love You!

How holy is your soul? Oh, Lord, I want to be holy, but it is so easy to give in when I am wronged. I do not mean to focus on myself and how I was hurt. I just do. Let me see that Your way is the way of the cross. When I am wronged, I must love my attackers. This is, oh, so hard, but Lord, I want to be holy. Give me Your grace and love because I of myself give in. Only through You can I act like You.

How holy is your soul? Lord, sometimes things just go wrong. People get irritable. I get tired. I get impatient. I want my way in my time. Lord, and then here comes my brother, demanding his way, and I don't want to listen. Lord, help me to put myself aside and be as You would want me to be. This I cannot do on my own. Give me, Lord, Your love and grace.

Lord, Lord, the way to You is hard. Give me the eyes to go beyond my human comprehension and see with Your eyes that which You want me to do. Help me to act with patience, love and peace that which I cannot do of myself. Give me Your love and peace so I can act as You desire me to.

The way to You, Lord, is hard for me. When I was hungry, Lord, You fed me. Please feed me Your love. Give me all I need to do this work for You. Of myself, Lord, I cannot act as You wish me to. Help me, Lord. Help me!

As I Am in My Soul, So I Will Shine to the World

R. As I am in this world, I must be as He wants me to be. When I dress, I must dress to please Him, not to draw attention to myself and my body, not to make myself a luring instrument, but to be dressed as the precious creation of God the Father. He has created me with such specialness. I am the way He wants me. I do not have to change my exterior or improve on the beauty He has given me. Beauty comes from within. Beauty comes from the love of God that shines from my face. Beauty is not beheld by my hair color or color of my lips. Beauty is seen in the eyes that reflect the soul.

Oh, how is my soul? How is my heart? My body is perfect. It was created by God the Father. I may have worn it for some years, but He loves me as I am. I must accept myself as I am and love myself as I am. My job is to wear the clothes of God the Father. He has adorned me perfectly well. I must work on my interior, not my exterior. That is what shows the real beauty! The body reflects the person within. So, as I am in my soul, I will shine to the world.

Lord, let me let go of my attachments to make my body my primary focus and focus on the heart and the things of the soul.

Jesus, Jesus, I love Thee!

I Give You My Life

Oh, beloved of My Father, I give you My life. My life I give to you, My precious one. If they only knew what they hold in their breasts. I am your treasure, little one. I am truly God. I speak to you. I lament their passing. They do not know that they hold Jesus Christ, the Son of God in their breasts. Tell them for Me, My child, tell them. Do not think of yourself, think of those moments we share every day after Communion and know My aching Heart. I am God. I come to them. Tell them I want to be, oh, so much closer with them, deeply in love with them.

Such indifference, such disrespect! They are blind. I am God. Listen to Me. I come to you in your body. Reverence Me. I beg you, do not wound Me with your blindness. I will make all things clear in your sight if you sit with Me. Don't just put in your time. You are here in deepest love with Me, yearning, loving, burning love. You run from My altar. I tell you I am God. You are My beloved ones.

Oh, I can't make you understand. You will not listen. You want your will. You want your word. You are so blind and so worldly dumb. I am truly here, Jesus Christ, the Son of God, Who died for you. What do I do to tell you? You do not listen. You do not, in your stiff-necked ways, comprehend My love, poured to you in the Eucharist! Come unto Me, beloved of My Father. I beg you to open your hearts to the fire of My love.

R. He allows me to experience His emotions to a small degree.

When you love someone, sweet one, you share that person's sorrow. I suffer for My beloved ones not to even realize they receive God truly present in the Eucharist.

R. I saw Jesus in a white tunic with a cross on His back. His gown was not really very stained. I saw His crown of thorns. I knew Mary was off to the side and He was looking into her eyes. I felt such sadness. I could see it as plainly as if I were there and experienced the emotion. (Saw in my heart,experienced emotion).

He told me to kneel in front of the tabernacle and praise Him, the one, true God, to soothe His Heart for all of His beloved ones who ran out after Communion. He told me to kneel three times.

After Communion I felt as if my entire chest was full and burning but I felt sadness because He was sad for those who had left. His white tunic was limp and somewhat dirty with dark mud. It was close to the beginning of when He had the cross because He appeared to have some strength. The day was bright and hot. The cross was big and not like a tree, as if it had been made with care.

How is it that Jesus - to make a cross with care for our beloved Savior? What of the minds and hearts of the men who had fashioned His cross? Did they think of what they were doing? Did they even know? What of the indifference and neglect we give to Jesus in Holy Communion? Do we even know? Do we realize that Jesus, the Son of God, waits for us with such longing as we walk away, that He is truly the same Jesus Who died this brutal death on the cross? Are we like those who fashioned His cross with care, not knowing what would become of such a cross?

Are our intentions pure, but we still wrong our brothers as we wrong Jesus when we treat Him with this irreverence before and after Communion? How do we become aware and tuned in to Jesus to know all He is making so clear?

We must listen. He is indeed speaking here. The Holy Spirit gives us His gifts that, where we were blind, we now see. Open our eyes to You, oh, blessed Savior. Let us see, with the eyes of God, all we are so blinded to. Just like this indifference to You is the way we treat our brothers. We do not even know we are neglectful and hurting them!

Open your hearts to the love of God. Beg for the gifts of the Holy Spirit. In loving Me, you love the Father. He loves you as I love you. We are one with each other. You are so loved, child, loved by Us. Think of a toddler that is given such love by its parents. We love you beyond your comprehension.

Mary, your mother, is forever by you. You are so loved. Be not blind. Angels and saints walk with you. You have the love of the one, triune God, child, and my own mother. She mothers you, child, no less than she mothered Me. Do not worry for your lives. Our love is surrounding you. You are so favored and blessed, and you fume and fret and go to the world!

Open your eyes and see with your hearts, all that is before you. You need intimacy in your hearts with the one, true God! We are one in you and you will be one in Us. Come and sup with Me, little one. The time is at hand. I give you a land flowing with milk and honey and you run for the barren desert.

Come, come to Me, My babies. You are so loved!

Do Not Walk from Me

I want you to kneel after Communion. I want you to kneel to comfort My aching Heart for those who leave with Me in their breasts. I am God. I am the same Jesus Who walked this earth. I want praise. I want adoration. I want honor. I want reverence. I want to be proclaimed God within your very body and revered with such honor.

This offends My aching Heart so, to have people leave minutes after I come to them. Tell them. I will tell you every day. I want you to speak out. It is with such ignorance that they leave. They do not know. You must tell them that I am God. I am Jesus, truly present, Body and Blood, Soul and Divinity, in their breast.

My veil will be broken. You will know that I am the Almighty God, truly present in the Eucharist. I am the Son of Man. I want this message to be preached, how I, God, am ardently awaiting their love in Communion. This is the gift of My love. I give Myself to you and you leave. I will tell you every day, if I have to, until you speak. I want this preached so people will realize that this is the great gift I give to them, that this is your treasure. The Holy Eucharist is My

Body and Blood. Tell them, tell them, tell them. They do such things because they are blind. I am the Almighty God and I come to you with such love.

I want reverence and honor and respect. I want love. I want your love. I come to you with love. I want your love in return. Please pay attention. This is wounding My aching Heart. People are not aware that I, Jesus Christ, Who suffered so, am no less present in the Eucharist. I love you so. I love them so. I beg you to preach this.

My little ones, such a gift to receive: the Son of God in your breast! And where I am, so are My Father and the Holy Spirit. This is the gift of love. Receive Me, come and sup with Me. I am God and I give Myself to you. Whatever you do after Communion is nothing compared to this gift. The gift I give is Myself. I love you so, little ones. Please spread this message. Your brothers do not know. They are blind. I love them so. I want to be united with them. They must sit with Me. I am God. I am truly present here. If I stood here, would you walk away? I come to you in your body. This is true intimacy! Do not walk from Me. I want this preached. The gift I give is Myself. I love you so!

May 24, 1994 After Communion at St. Gertrude Church
The Heart

You can turn your hearts off. The heart connects with the soul. You know Me in your heart. To turn your hearts off is to tune Me out. You must be free in your feelings with Me. There must be a flow of openness between Me and you. We connect in our hearts. Your heart must be pure. Anger, resentment, hatred and sin block the line that goes to the heart. You must be free of sin and anger which keep you closed to Me. A heart of God is free from anger. You must forgive and love one another. This keeps your lines open.

My grace flows from My Heart to your heart. We are joined in our hearts. I am one in you. You are one in Me. To be joined to My Heart and the Heart of Mary, you must be pure, any anger discarded. You should constantly be cleaning your heart. Staying connected to God keeps your heart pure. I give you such grace and love when you come to Me. I fill your heart with Me, and you are made whole in My love.

The heart is the way to Me. You stay connected to each other in your hearts. You must love one another. He who is not of the heart is alone. Let go with your heart, filled with My love! Be free, get rid of your sins, forgive and love. Be pure. Keep your souls white. Live in the truth. Strive in all things to be holy. You are not perfect. It is your job to confess your sins and be truthful. Have genuine sorrow for all that you do that is wrong.

Pray for the vision of God. You are so unaware of how you sin, of what you do that is so unloving. Pray for vision in your heart to know God and know His ways. You must pray to the Holy Spirit to make you wise in the ways of the Lord. See, little ones, with your hearts. See with the eyes of God. Beg to see more clearly what He wants you to see. Compassion, love, kindness, gentleness, giving. You are so caught up in your world and your wills. Pray to the Father to know and to do His Will.

I am Jesus, the Son of God. I come to you that you will have life and have it more abundantly. God is life. God is love. God is here for you this day. Open wide the gates and enter into His court. Praise His name. Worship and glorify Him for He is so great and worthy of all praise. He is God. You are so favored! Pray for vision!

Pray to see with your hearts. Your eyes are not that by which you know God. I work inside your hearts. Go inside yourselves, go to your hearts, set them free with love. Hatred and anger keep them bound up. Release the bonds that tie your hearts. Satan tries to squeeze the life from your hearts. He is heartless. He wants your hearts to wither and die. Nurture your heart with My love. Feed your hearts with the Eucharist. I am the gift of love. You come, I give Myself to you. I fill you with the bread of life. You are made whole in Me. Oh, it is so simple! You make things so hard! Do not let your hearts become hard. Feed them My love and they will grow in the love of God.

Do not let your hearts turn cold, warm them with the fire of My love. I am on fire for love of you. I am the Sacred Heart of Jesus. I am God. I am waiting for you, My beloved. Come and join yourself to Me!

May 25, 1994 After Communion at All Saints Church   **7:10a.m.**

You Are Surrounded by Angels

R. You are God, Father, Son and Holy Spirit. I bow before You.

You, My child, have received the one, true God. Every knee should bend and be in reverence. If you could behold the sight of what surrounds you at My presence! Angels are surrounding you. Praise you, for God is with you, Father, Son and Holy Spirit. Mary, My mother, is with you. Are you ever so honored to behold the Son of God within your breast? Praise Him, the holiest in the heights. God comes to you and is truly within you! If you could behold beyond this veil, you would radiate such light and power. You, My child, are so unaware of Me within your breast. You do not see. You are blind. I am God. I am within you. Bow to Me, My child, when you come. You should scarcely be able to walk. I am God and you behold Me! Praise Me. Worship Me. Angels surround you.

I am God. Do you even know? Such indifference to Me, such love poured out to you. I am God! You are so caught up in your silly things and you run, with God still in your bodies, for what things?

If the veil were lifted, you would see My might. You would fall to the floor and praise Me. You are so blind. How do I tell you, little ones?

Behold, the Son of God enters you in such a great gift of love! God is within you. Where God is, so is the Father and Holy Spirit, for we are one. Oh, harken to Me, pray to know what you do not know, pray to the Holy Spirit. Pray to your Father, pray to Mary. I am Jesus and I come to you with such love! I am the one, true God!

R. We are trying to fix God into our world. He is the Almighty God. He is first. He has all the power. The reverence for God has gone out of our religion.

Bow down before the altar. Kiss the floor. Worship Me. I am God. Behind the tabernacle doors I am still God. People do not comprehend that God Is truly present! What is more important than God being with you and waiting for you in church? Oh, My children, you are blind. Your world is a passing thing. I am God and I am in your midst this day the same as the day I walked on Calvary! You are so blind.

Open your hearts. Pray for the gifts of the Holy Spirit to know these truths. You need God, My little ones. You need the one, triune God, Father Son, Holy Spirit! Pray to Us, ask your mother to guide you, to help you to love Me as she loves Me. She loves God with the purest Heart. Love Jesus through Mary's sinless Heart. Love God through the Immaculate Heart of Mary.

R. How can I, such a sinner, love God? But, to be joined to Mary's Heart, I can love with her sinless Heart. She loves God and her Heart is immaculate. I want a holy heart. I must join with Mary's Heart. It is all pure!

I have a sinful heart. How do I love God as He should be loved? Go through Mary's pure Heart!

We do not even know how we offend the Lord. He is as He is. He is the Almighty God. He deserves such reverence and honor and praise. The world has turned godless. He is the one, true God. The problem is with the world.

I am the Almighty God. I ardently love you. My greatest gift to you is Myself. I give you Myself in the Eucharist. This is far greater than any supernatural symbol. I am Jesus Christ, the risen Lord, and I come to you in the Blessed Sacrament. The power is in the Eucharist. I am truly present there. I am God and I am in your midst. I am treated with such unimportance. You don't even know how you offend Me. You are judging My importance by this godless society. The world is being dominated by Satan. Come to Me in the Eucharist. The power is in the Eucharist!

You see the sun spin and you cry, "Oh, God, God." He is in the Eucharist, the risen Lord. "Oh, God, My God." Think of your joy to behold something supernatural. You fall to your knees in awe. God is here!

R.So much power in the Eucharist. I couldn't touch it, it is under the veil.

(I asked Jesus to come to me through the sinless Heart of Mary. I felt the Father above, the Holy Spirit, in union with Jesus, through the Immaculate Heart of Mary.)

Mary speaks:

You, my child, are being taught. You grow in your relationship with God. My way is to lead you to my Son. You will continue to grow in your closeness with God. Your life is your journey to be united with Him more and more. Do not feel anxious for not knowing all at once. You grow each minute of each day in your knowledge and love of God. Do not be anxious about your growth. Be open to what He sends you this moment. Place your heart in His hands and be united to Him. Let go.

Praise God and be at peace. Your heart will grow when you are at peace. You are learning the truths about God. You are growing each day in your love of Him. I am your mother. Thank you for responding to my call.

The Crucifixion

Mary speaks:

As tenderly as I beheld my beautiful Son in my arms, and with such love, I watched His death on the cross with great anguish, my Heart torn apart by the sight of Him, hanging in such pain! I could hardly stand it! I was held up by my beloved John. Joy and pain—the pain to behold Him and His suffering, the joy to know your salvation was won through His blood!

Such lamenting! I could not cry deeply enough for the anguish I felt. His Blood was spent. His life was given. He did this, my child, for love of you. I am your mother. I love you, my precious ones. I love you as I love my beautiful Son, Jesus.

I am Mary, your beloved mother. Call to me. I know of your sufferings. I will comfort you. I suffered for love of you. You are so precious to Us. Live in the love of my Son. He is with you this day in the Eucharist. I am Mary, your mother. Thank you for responding to my call.

Be Not Afraid

My dear child, do not fear. Come to Me and receive My peace. Do you think I would write to you all this time and not protect you? This will make you stronger in your love of Me. You are My love. I am using you to do this work and I will protect you as My beloved. You do this totally out of love of Me.

I am Jesus Christ, Son of the Living God. Listen sweet one, totally trust in My love. I truly love you. My relationship with you depends on faith and trust. We love each other. Do not be afraid. I am God and I walk with you wherever you go.

I am the Lord, thy God. Harken to Me and receive My peace.

Be Loving to Your Children

R. I hurt you, my little child, when I lashed back at you. I didn't see you suffering. I only knew you hurt me and I wanted you to know why you should never hurt me. I saw you, my little child, walk away with your head bowed down. I was not feeling good inside to see you suffering from my words. Oh, sweet one, I love you. I did not want to hurt you. I didn't know how angry my tongue can be and play out my hurt when you are hurting and need my love. The worst was to watch you, little one, walk away in the school yard with your head so bowed down. I am so sorry for hurting you, my beloved little child!

It is so hard to spread Christ's love when you are wronged. I knew that I could have cast out the devil, but I thought I would tell you what you needed to know. I should never respond to you, my little child, with anger. God wants to teach you His love through me. How can He love if I react with anger to you? The worst was to see I made you suffer. You, with your little head bowed down in the school yard, and you had to go to school and sit there all day.

What I did to you I did to Jesus. I see Jesus walking along at Calvary, His head bowed down. I see Him being led away after His scourging, His head bowed down. I see Him after He is crowned, His head bowed down.

How often have I led You away, Jesus, when I hurt my brothers? Do You put Your head down and suffer silently for my sins?

To see the hurt that I caused you and others is surely an awakening. It hurts me worse to realize how I have hurt any person and how my hurting you has hurt Christ Himself, my beloved child, my beloved Jesus!

Teach me Your ways, oh, precious Lord, to see the hurt I cause my children and my brothers with neglect or anger, or just ignorance. Teach me to know Your ways, to see the eyes of God, the whole picture, to see the others as You do, to know their suffering in their hearts, to not give in to myself and offend You more. I see the bowed down face of Jesus as He walked away, persecuted and scorned, hurt and bleeding, led away in silence.

Let me love, Lord. Of myself, I cannot do this. Oh, my God, help me to know Your ways and follow in Your footsteps, to be silent when I am attacked, not to give in to the self to justify and condemn, to be as You desire me to be.

Let me love, Lord. The way to You is love, love when I am being persecuted, love when I want to give in and fight back, love, love, love. Only love keeps my heart open or You close to me!

Let me never see a person walk from me bowed down from my words. Forgive me for my anger. Of myself, Lord, I cannot do this. You are my strength. Holy Spirit, open my eyes to see my brother as you desire me to see him, not from my side, but from Your side.

Alleluia. And He imparted to them His gifts and they learned in their errors how more fully to surrender to the Lord and let Him operate their hearts. Alleluia. He opened their eyes and their hearts, and they saw how they could love their brothers.

For Children

R. God asks us for two things: to love Him and to love one another. People hurt and they act nastily. They need our love. They do not need us to fight with them. Jesus' way is to love. We will enter heaven on how we loved God and loved one another.

He takes care of us. We have a loving Father and a loving

mother. She mothers us as she mothered Jesus. She is always by our side. Jesus is always by our side. The more I learn to love Jesus, the more I love the Father.

Sometimes our parents suffer and are upset. Pray for them. God loves little children. Unless we love like little children, we won't enter into heaven. Little children have big hearts. They are so close to Jesus.

He loves you to pray to Him. He waits for you. He is the very same Jesus Who died on the cross. He wanted to stay with you so He instituted the sacrament of the Eucharist. Jesus comes to tell you He is with you this day in church and in the Eucharist.

He would die today for you alone. He loves you this much! He loves you. He can love you and be personal with you and have love for someone else at the same time because He is God.

The love of Jesus led Him to die for you, so you could one day go to heaven. He loves you so much He died for you and gave the last beat of His Heart and the last drop of His blood for you.

He longs and waits for you to come and be with Him in Communion. He wants to be your best friend. He wants you to love Him first. Then you will love your father and mother and sisters and brothers better also.

Pray to the Holy Spirit to know and love God. The Holy Spirit will change your life if you pray to Him. He is God. He has all knowledge and He loves you.

Mary suffered, as Jesus suffered, for love of you. She has a sinless Heart. If you pray to Mary, if you love God through her Heart, she will help you to love God.

May 28, 1994 Before Mass

Listen to Me

My little one, I write, you listen. Listen, child. Do you know how to listen to Me? Constant talking, noise, constant—do you listen? I am God, child. I know all things, yet you go on and on. I know your heart. I know your every thought and desire before you ever do. You do too much. My way is surrender. Let go into the arms of Jesus. See yourself fall from the highest mountain with no fear in your heart.

This is how you must let go to Me. Come in silence. Do not control your time with Me. One hour of total uninterrupted adoration! Let it happen as the Holy Spirit prompts you to be with God.

Listen. Be silent. You do not hear because you do not listen. You control your time. You do what you want. It is My hour. I give to you. You come and be with Me and let go of it all. Let it happen. Let God plan the hour. Why are you telling Me so many things? Do you think I do not know?

If you tell Me, because you need Me to listen, I listen, but you need not tell Me some things. When you love someone there is a knowing of each other's ways. You understand such things. I know all things. I am God. I ardently love you. I know from whence you come and where you are going. I know you. I knew you from birth. I know your end. I know you in your eternity. You see minutes, you see seconds, you see like a human. I know your life to come. Let go, child. Come to Me and lay yourself before Me. Open wide and let Me have full reign in your hearts. I know you and love you so.

Why do you worry so? Why worry at all? I am God. I know all things and I am watching out for you. Oh, My beloved one, if you could see how blind you are!

Listen and be taught. Open to Me. Surrender to Me in all things. Your time is better spent in total surrender to Me. Your time is My time. Let Me plan your time. Surrender entirely to Me.

I love you, My precious child! This is Jesus, Son of the Living God. Let Me live in you. Surrender to Me and My way. I love you.

You Are My Baby

I want to write to you and talk to you like My little baby. I love you so, sweet one. See your body. I love your body as it is. You are My baby. I love you just as you are, beautiful creation of My Father. Love yourself as you are. You are so loved by God, Father, Son and Holy Spirit, and your beautiful mother. I love you. I love you. I love you, child. Know how I guard your every step, like a baby. I watch you walk and I love to watch you. You are so loved, little baby, beloved of mine. Want for no love or attention for I am giving you everything you need.

You come from a place of being full. When you are complaining, read this note. You are not realizing the immense love God has for you. Oh, sweet little one, I love you so. Circulate this letter to My beloved ones. I love each precious one just this way.

R. I can finally be the little child. After all the years I took care of my own children, I am now free. God takes care of me. He wants me to be a baby and be dependent on Him. This is freedom, to be faced with a big obstacle and say, "Here, Lord, You take it."

My job is to be the light shining in the dark world. My job is to shed His love on others. My job is to turn it over to Him and love for Him. My job is to accept His Will this day for me and know, whatever I receive, He is giving out of ardent love for me.

Oh, how I love You, my Lord. Alleluia. He is so good to us. He is our refuge and our strength. He is our Savior. We are His. We are His. We were created by God, the Father. He is our Father. Mary is our mother. We are His. We were created to know, love and serve Him. We are but little babies at the breast. This is true freedom, true freedom. Unless we become as little children, we cannot enter the kingdom of heaven. Oh, what a gift! What freedom! Oh, I love You so, my God, Father, Son and Holy Spirit.

Babies goes to their parents for all their needs. When they are hurt, they go to their parents. When I am hurt, I go to You. You are God. You can do all things! I become totally dependent on You. I am the baby. I know You have all I need. You are a real Person. It is in trials that I am drawn closer to God. I must trust in Him, alleluia, for His love!

May 28, 1994 After Mass at All Saints Church   **5:30p.m.**

Jesus Is Truly Present

You must tell your friends Jesus is truly present! At Saturday and Sunday masses, they are so irreverent. Please tell your friends to say, "Jesus is truly present. Reverence Him, please. God is here and in our midst." Do not fear. You are doing this for Me.

I am so wounded by this irreverence. Tell your friends to kneel after Communion when they pray. This wounds My aching Heart. I want to be honored as God.

People do not even talk to Me. They receive Me and leave church. I am so offended! With such love I come and give Myself to them! If they could truly see Me, they would not be able to see. Tell them. Tell all about My Real Presence!

Kneel before My tabernacle, it pleases Me so. I will protect your knees. I love you to adore Me. I am the Sacred Heart of Jesus. I am truly present here, Body and Blood, Soul and Divinity.

May 28, 1994 After Mass

I Guard You with Tender Love

It is in suffering that I am closest to you. It is in your trials that you learn My lessons. No person has any power over you. I am Jesus Christ, the Son of God. It is for love of all that I write to you and it is for love of each person that I will see that they receive My messages.

I am the Son of God. Do not fear for I am your rear guard and your fore guard. I bear you up lest you dash your foot against a stone. I write here to you, My precious one. Your job is to focus on Me and My intense love. You are being taught constantly. Accept all things I give to you with My deepest love. I guard you with the tenderest love. Let go of all of your life and be My empty vessel to receive My message.

I am God. No one has any power over Me. I am writing to give My loved ones My love. I will see to the distribution of My letters. Any snags you receive immediately give to Me. You do not have to handle anything but praying to Me and doing My Will. My Will is to be united to you and teach you each lesson so lovingly. Oh, sweet one, how dearly I love you. I love you so intently. Be alone with Me and let Me be with you in your heart.

My mother is with you. She will teach you to love through her Heart. The Father and Holy Spirit are with you. So intense is this love of God! Your mother is Mary. Your Father is God. What do you, child, have to fear? Be as a baby. Love, love, love and receive the love of your Father and mother.

I am Jesus, the Son of God. Come and lay yourself in My Heart. You are swallowed up inside of My Heart and protected with such love. I am your Beloved One. Come to Me and feel My intense love for you, My beloved.

R.Jesus, Jesus! Though the earth be shaken and the stars cease to shine, Your light is ever upon us. You shine as a beacon light in the darkest night. Your power is endless.

I came to you, My beloved child, and I gave you strength to know that I control all things. You are never to doubt or be afraid for I walk before you this walk in this valley of tears. You are My child. You do not walk alone. You walk with Me, My precious one. I am Jesus, your Savior. I sustain you.

Not one letter of My law will pass away. I go before you and you are led down My path, by My bushes and flowers, thistles and rocks. But I lead, you must follow. Some are thorny, some are fragrant. You must take the bad with the good. I sustain you, My beloved one.

When they persecute you and holler every slander against you, look to My battered body. My blood was given for you. My flesh was torn. Your cross is so little, My child. You do not worry. Cast all doubt away. I am He Who sustains you. I love you. Do you believe I love you? You must let go now and see Me with My beautiful face and white tunic. I am all gentleness and love. I am God. See Me, child. See My face and My whole body standing next to you. Feel My presence in this room.

May 29, 1994 Before Mass

Trinity Sunday

I am with you, My precious one. I am God. Today is the Feast of the Trinity. God is here, Father, Son and Holy Spirit. Praise Us, worship Us, honor Us. We are truly present and ready to take your prayers to Our heavenly court.

After Communion:

The more you know and love Me, the more you know and love the Father, for He is one in Me and I am one in Him. The Father has sent Me to be one in you. Reach with love in your heart for the one, triune God. To know Me is to love the Father. He is your Father. He created you. He loves you. You are His precious creation.

The Holy Spirit is the love that exists between the Father and Son. It is through the Spirit you are given the knowing power to see God. God is one, Father, Son and Holy Spirit, three equal persons in one God. Go to the Spirit. Beg for His gifts to see God, one, holy, true. Go to the Spirit. Ask Him to remove the blinders from your eyes. Where you were blind, you now see. You see with such clarity, you hear with such wisdom, only through the Spirit. You of yourself would not know such things. Beg to be opened to the Spirit. Beg Him to give you His life within you.

Love your Savior Jesus Christ and know how He loves you through the Eucharist. Know that all the love you have for Jesus and He has for you is extended to the Father for they are one with each other.

If you could behold the sight of God, your eyes could not see. You do not reach with your hearts to know God. Pray to the Spirit to open up your hearts and give you the eyes to see. You of yourself are blind and deaf. This is the gift of the Spirit, to know God. Such love pours out to you. Pray to Mary to love through her sinless Heart.

R. God in His magnificence is truly present. How do I love Him? How do I, a mere creature, love God? Only through the Immaculate Heart of Mary can I love with such great love. My precious God, I am so imperfect. Through her sinless Heart, through her ardent love for God, I can love Him more deeply.

Spirit, open my eyes. Fill me. Open my heart. Give me Your life that the life and love of God might dwell within my breast. I beg for Your gifts. I implore You to help me unite more fully with God through Mary.

And I came unto you and you were filled with My love, and the power of the Lord shone upon you, the power of the the one, tri-une God.

R.He is mighty and worthy of all praise. Fall to your knees. Fall and adore Him. Alleluia. Alleluia.

Jump for Joy That Jesus Calls You

My precious one, I called in the night. You did not answer My call. You must obey Me. This displeases Me. I call, you come. You must not give into yourself. Once you are awake, you are not tired. Jump from your bed and run to My arms, My beloved. Do not ever not answer My knocking. Jump, child, jump for joy that Jesus calls you in the night. I want you in the night, you sleep, you miss My time with you. Forget your sleep. You are tired from sleeping. When I call, I want you to come now!

I am your God. Harken to My pleading to be close to you. I want you to let go of your distractions and be totally alone with Me. The past is over, the future is to come. Surrender your present moments to Me. I will care for all your needs. Do not belabor the past. Come to Me with your sorrow. I am God and I want to love you.

I will fill you. I will comfort you. I will love you. Deepen this dependence on Me. I never change. I am steadfast in My love and I wait for you to come to Me. I wait for you like a doting mother. I am God, child. All the love you crave I have to give and pour out to you. I want to shower you with love.

Love others no matter what they say and do. They need My love through you. They need My love freely given from you.

I pour Myself out to you. Love your fellows if they love you or if they hate you. Love them as I love you. To My death I loved you.

It is good to exchange love with your beloved ones, but give your love freely. Do not love to expect love back. Love to love your brothers. If they love you in return, you are receiving My love through them. This is good for you but do not expect their love in return. Give freely to your brother. To give love, My love is uncondi-tional. There are no strings on My love. It is given freely to all. All My people are My beloved ones. I would die for each soul this very day. Love all your brothers for Me.

My beloved one, pray for this love. You cannot of yourself love the way I call you to. You must spend time with Me, when I pour My love out to you, so you have it to give. You need silence with Me. This is the key to your life, to spend time alone with God. You are restored and refueled in these quiet moments.

You Need the Holy Spirit

My child, I love you so much. I want you to be alone with Me at night. Jump from your bed and be with Me. Receive Me in the early hours. I love to be alone with you.

Your life is so short, sweet one. You will soon see how you are preparing yourself for the days ahead. No preparation is enough. Times will be hard times. Such a false peace exists. Children will be guarded. I am a just God. I love My little ones. Parents will be led back to God and His world. Where they were blind, they now see.

Pray constantly for souls. Do not think that you can be at rest. You need to be constantly about preaching My word and praying for your brothers' souls. Their souls are at stake!

The Eucharist is the center to draw men's hearts back to God. Promote the Real Presence. Tell everyone how I am Jesus Christ, the Son of God, and I truly give Myself to them in the Eucharist.

Tell them to pray to the Holy Spirit. Tell children about the Holy Spirit. The Holy Spirit is full of gifts. You will know God through Him. His fire and life He gives to you and the life of God is alive in your soul. Pray to Him. Tell all about the Spirit. He must be alive in your hearts to know God. Tell all to pray to Him. It is through His gifts your eyes will be opened and you will see things only God can show you.

R. Such simplicity! Take the wisdom of God—so simple, but so profound. Where I was blind, I now can see. Enkindle in me Your gifts, Spirit of God. Where I once was dead, I have become filled with Your life. You breathed Your life deep into my soul and I could see clearly as never before.

Such wisdom! Such profound truths! You reveal to me with such simplicity! Oh,man of himself is so blind and the Spirit is so alive! Enkindle in me Your life. The deaf hear, the blind see. The life of God is enkindled in our hearts and we know the fire that burns deep in our breast, a fire of love for our precious God, three in one, Father, Son and Holy Spirit. Such love for You, my God! You are one with Jesus. Such immense love I have for You and You have for us. Where I was blind, I now can see. Your word I love, Your Mass I love, You I love. My God, three in one,

and holy, holy is Your name! I bow before You with such reverence at Your might. You are mighty and worthy of all honor and
praise and holy, holy is Your name, one triune God, Father, Son
and Holy Spirit! I bow low and reverence You in Your might. I
kiss the ground and give You homage. You are holy and holy is
Your name. I praise You. I worship You. I bow before You, God,
Father, Son and Holy Spirit!

"Where I was blind, I now see." For quite a while I have been
getting this, constantly, all day long. "Where I was blind, now I
see." What do I see? I see God as never before through the Holy
Spirit. There is burning and life in my breast for I love God, three
in one, so dearly. The Holy Spirit removes the blinders from our
eyes. We see the word of God as never before. Our hearts know
God. We read His word and participate at the Mass with such joy
and love, to participate in every word, to know as we did not
know before, to read the word. To go to Mass and love God, we
need the wisdom, understanding and knowledge of the Holy
Spirit. It is His Spirit alive in our hearts that makes the Mass
come alive in such color and it grows daily in our hearts.

Spirit, pour Yourself into me. Give me Your life. I am on fire
with the love of God. The more You give me, the more I see.
Where I was blind, I now can see! See with the eyes of God.
Take my blinders from my eyes, impart to me wisdom to know
as only God knows, knowledge to know God, understanding to
grasp the meaning of Your truths, love, enkindled and burning
so brightly deep within my breast. You are the one, true God,
Father, Son and Holy Spirit. Give me the life and love of God
that flows from the Spirit alive in me. Enkindle in me fire for
my God!

I ardently love my beloved Jesus and I know more His love
for me. I know more fully the love of Jesus through the spirit
alive in my breast. Jesus is one with the Father. The love He
has for me comes from the Father. The Father created us. He
loves us so. He willed His only Son to die that we might have
eternal life. All the love I have for Jesus and He has for me is
enkindled in my heart for my dear, loving Father. What a
Father to behold! I can scarcely speak, realizing a little of His
great love for me. This I realize through my love of Jesus. Oh,
how I love my beloved Jesus. My heart burns inside, but to
magnify this love with the love of the Father and the Holy
Spirit, I can scarcely speak.

I receive Jesus in Communion. I receive God! The one, triune
God is present. Where Jesus is, so is His beloved mother. She

loves us so. She suffered for us. She is the Immaculate Heart of Mary. It is through her sinless Heart I learn to love my God. My love is so imperfect. Her love is so pure. She is the daughter of the Father, the mother of the Son, the spouse of the Holy Spirit. Such love she has for God. Through her pure Heart, I can give love to my beloved God more abundantly.

The road is not visible to some, only to those who see with the eyes of faith, for you never trod alone.

To see as You want us to see and not as we want to see, give us Godly vision, Lord. I am grasping for the love of God and Mary. I pray to know God more fully and love Him through my beloved mother. Oh, how I am in awe and my heart is burning for this love of God.

I am given such life through the Holy Spirit. This growth is constant. I love the Mass, I love the word of God! I am so excited for this life I feel within me. Give me Your eyes to see. Where I was blind, I now see and what do I behold when the blinders are removed? The one, true, magnificent God, holy and true and in our midst this very day through Jesus in the Eucharist.

Bow down, bend low, behold it is God among us. Where I was blind, I now can see. Praise You, Spirit, for Your life within my soul. May Your fire ever grow within me and radiate Your love to this world.

Alleluia. Praise the one, true God! What I am seeing is not with eyes. It is in my heart. A blind man can see more in his heart than his faithful ones see with their eyes.

June 1, 1994

How Do You See God in Me?

R. He is calling us to cheerfulness. If I saw myself through some other person's eyes, would I see God or would I see a perplexed person without peace?

Lord, let me see myself as You see me. Do I display the peace of Christ in my soul or do I display the uneasiness that Satan tries to produce inside me?

Oh, Lord, how am I preaching Your gospel to my children? Do I complain before prayer and in the car or am I cheerful and showing them how anxious I am to be with You? What do I teach my children about my love of You?

Lord, where I am blind, open my eyes. Oh, Spirit of God, impart to me Your gifts: wisdom, understanding, knowledge to know You more, my sweet and precious God, to realize the immense love of God and be filled by it, to let go of the perishable things of the world and see, with eyes as never before, what is so important to You—my love poured out to my children, my love for all, which is Your love deep within me, Your love that is too powerful to be contained and is given to all those I am with.

Help Me to Carry My Crosses Without Complaint

R. Do I complain? Do I take my troubles to Jesus and show you His love? Is it not my job here to love? Why do I need to tell you my sorrow? Is it not given as a gift from my Beloved One to draw me closer to His arms? When I burden you with my sorrow, I miss the opportunity to share it with Him Who truly cares and knows exactly what I feel.

Oh, Jesus, impart to me a new heart, a heart filled with such love for my brothers as not to laden them with my cares, but to give them Your love. Let me have the strength to carry each load You give me as You carried Your cross on Calvary without complaint.

Let me walk my walk with You and give Your love to all those I meet. Oh, Jesus, You are so loving, to love me in all my imperfections, to want me in all my moods and always to be there with outstretched arms, waiting for me. Help me to carry my crosses with Your joy. I love You, my Savior.

The Good News

Fasting must come from a joyful heart. What good does it do you to fast and wear sack cloth and ashes? You must fast for love of Me and My mother. You are fasting for penance, for the intentions of Our Hearts. What good does it do you to fast and look glum.

Everything you do must come from a joyful heart. Be glad you are My chosen race. You know the good news. You are favored. Your heavenly Father loves you, I love you, the Holy Spirit loves you, you are mothered by My very own mother! I am Jesus Christ and I am in your midst this very day. You have an everlasting reward, paid for with My blood.

Think of having a friend that loved you so that He died for you! I am God and I was born a mere human and died a brutal death that you might have life eternal. Hearken to Me. I am by your side this day with such love for you. Spread the good news. Jesus Christ is Lord. He has died and He is risen that you might have life eternal. Alleluia.

You Know Not the Day or the Hour

Whatever you do, be of a clean heart. Do not be bound up in your heart. Let go of hate and anger. Free yourself of such chains. Anger tears at your heart and makes you glum. Be at peace. Have a heart of joy. My life I give to you. You are set on fire with the love of the one, triune God, Father, Son, Holy Spirit. Shout it from the housetops, raise the roofs, declare it on the streets. Jesus is Lord. He has died and He is risen for love of you, child. You are this loved and what awaits you is My home in heaven.

Be clean in your heart. Love God, love one another. The time is near, the place is set. You will be caught unawares. All that will sustain you is your relationship with God. Be ready, be watchful. You know not the day or the hour. By your love you will inherit My kingdom. Love all, old and young, black and white, burdened and happy. Your job is to spread the Good News. No earthly treasures will sustain you. You must stay close to God and follow His commandments. For I cried out to you and you were deaf. I sent My Spirit into your midst to give you vision and hearing. He filled you with such gifts you could scarcely speak and, where you were deaf and blind, you could see and hear. The Spirit imparts to you My vision. Pray with your hearts open. Beg for His gifts. Where you were blind, you now see. Alleluia. Alleluia.

Let Your Light Shine in the Darkness

My sweet one, you know I am here. Do you not feel such presence with you? I am your beloved Jesus, clothed in white and by your side. I come, I dwell in your heart. My love for you I pour into your heart. I love you so, My sweet child. Be open, for great things are to come. You will see as you never saw before. Where you were blind you now see. You feel such presence for I truly surround you. I am Jesus, your Precious One, the Sacred Heart of Jesus, come to be close to you, child.

Fear not, for I am with you. You have done as I requested. Dismiss your fears and be about My loving. You will see. Where you were blind, now you see. Oh, blessed of My Father, that you could behold such love poured out into your soul. Such yearning and longing I have for each soul. I want them to know of My love. Hold not back. It is through your recognition of My love for you that you will preach My love for all. My Heart is on fire, on fire! Preach this.

Do not be afraid. My presence surrounds you. My love I give you. You are My beloved one.

R. And there was light and the light shown brightest in the darkness. The nights were illuminated by the fire of this love, poured forth into the hearts of those who believed in Him Who is abundantly present to all.

Call out in a loud voice. Proclaim My words to the people. Stop at nothing to spread My glorious love. The glory is won in heaven. You are My messenger. You live not for this world, only to draw your brothers to My love, poured out in such abundance in the Eucharist. Come, My beloved ones, partake in My Body, given just for you. My life I give to you. Why are you so blind? Why do you hold on to such uselessness when I am truly present here this very day to you in such significance? My presence I make known to you. I am Jesus Christ, the Son of God. My love I pour out to you with such abundance. My Heart burns for you, My precious ones. Come to Me, let Me hold you in My Most Sacred Heart.

For you come and I am your God. I give you My life. Come, flock to My altar. Know that I, the one, triune God, am here this day and I await you with open arms to caress you. I love you so, My precious one. What do I do to tell you more?

Circulate this letter, give this message to all. Time is short. Souls are at stake and I am truly in your midst, your beloved Jesus. I wait. I long. I want you to come and share My love for I am Jesus Christ, your beloved One. Come, come, come to Me. Lead all to My Sacred Heart. Nothing has any reference except as it pertains to God. Give your brothers the gift of My words given directly to you.

I love you. I love you. I love them so!

June 8, 1994   6:15a.m.
Where We Were Blind We Now See

You search, you look, you wander, you ache, you find nothing. Oh, little one, when do you learn? You go to man to ask the things of God. Pray to the Spirit, beg Him for His gifts. No man knows what God alone knows. You will wander. You will seek. You will find nothing of what you need to know.

I will teach you My ways. I will support and comfort you. Creatures are as they are. They are imperfect, My little one. You must come to Me. I am truly here. It is your doubt that has caused you such anxiety. No one will confirm to you what I alone am telling you.

Where you were blind, My child, you now see. You learn your lessons. You are given trials. You suffer. But what lessons you learn that draw you close to Me!

I am talking to you, child. God! I know all things. I am talking in your heart. You go to man, you get answers from man. Go to God. Pray to the Spirit. He gifts you with wisdom, understanding, knowledge. You are strengthened in His love, love that He alone can give. Will you come to God with your heart open? Will you wait for His time? Will you accept your trials I so sweetly use to teach you? Will you be blind or will you see, not with eyes, child, but in your hearts, what you need to see?

Go to man, get things of man. Go to God to learn the things of God. No man knows what God wants to tell you in your heart.

R. Spirit of God, gift us with Your gifts. Give us all we need to know You, God, and to know Your Will for us. Strengthen us to follow You and not be led astray with a quick answer. Give us the fire of Your love!

You, God, are three in one, Father, Son and Holy Spirit. Three Persons, one God. Give us all we need to know, love and serve You in this world and draw others to You. Open our eyes. Where we were blind, we now see.

I will sustain you, I will reach down, I will lift you up, to such heights that only I can reach. You are reaching for the answers of God in the world. Go to God for your answers. I'm communicating to you in your heart this very day. I am God and you will know Me in your heart. Look inward, be in silence, pray to the Spirit to know.

June 9, 1994

I Will Sustain You

My child, let go of it all. You are making it hard on yourself. You need not worry for I will sustain you. Do you think I write all these letters and I will leave you in the lurch? Your strength is coming from this trial.

You do not need to worry ever. I am by your side. I am Jesus Christ, the Son of God. I come that you will have life. Such intimacy you will have with Me!

I am God. I will sustain you. You walk the way to Calvary with Me. My load is made lighter.

To Focus on Self Is Not of Me

The self is the enemy. When people promote themselves, they cease to be of Me. A person fixed in Me is selfless and unattached. The more you tend toward selflessness, the greater your union with Me. No man who is caught up in himself and his achievements is of Me.

Only as you lend yourself to My work, only as you give freely of yourself and come to Me, will you be made My mighty warrior.

The more you are focused on self, the more the devil plays on your ego. To promote yourself is not to promote Me!

A person fixed in My work denies the self and operates in humbleness. A person fixed in My work receives his answers from Me in front of the tabernacle. You cannot be of Me and be controlling. You do not control when I am operating you.

My ways are steadfast and direct. Your actions are rooted in your ardent love for Me, not promotion of yourself.

I am the Way. I am the Truth. I am the Life. He who abides in Me will have the light of life.

I Am the Sacred Heart of Jesus

R. This is the feast of the Sacred Heart. Oh, my Jesus, I give You such proclamation of joy on Your feast day.

I am the Sacred Heart of Jesus. I am ablaze for love of you this very day. I come to you and you are filled with My fire. My Heart is an endless furnace of My love.

Do you realize My power, My little one? Do you know I am God and you have nothing to fear? You focus so on Satan's distractions and I watch you and want you to let go and find refuge from your pain in My Heart.

I am the Sacred Heart of Jesus. I am Jesus, the Son of God. Nothing happens that I do not allow. You are forgetting My intense might. I am the Sacred Heart of Jesus. I come and you are filled with such splendor!

Take Up the Cup of Salvation

I ask you, My beloved ones, to suffer for souls. Time is so short. Some of your brothers will lose their souls. You must accept your sufferings, My faithful ones. I ask you to pick up your crosses. Life in Me is through the cross.

Your brothers' souls are at stake. Will you suffer for the sake of your brothers? Will you love your brothers as I love you?

Take up the cup of salvation. Realize My crown is not a crown of splendor. It is a crown of thorns. Your life here is passing. Your time is short. Your suffering and prayers can help save souls. Pray the Divine Mercy. Pray the rosary and meditate on My Passion.

Suffer with Me for the sake of your beloved brothers. Your life should be spent to draw your brothers to heaven. When you act, they are learning My ways from you. Do you want your brothers to have life forever in heaven? You must love when they persecute you. Think of their souls. You must accept your crosses without complaint. Accept them with joy and find refuge in My most Sacred Heart.

Come to My Heart for your love. I will refuel you, My beloved child. You cannot do it without My love. Rest in My Heart, dear one. I am the Sacred Heart of Jesus. My Heart is on fire for love of you. Come and be filled with My love. Accept your suffering. The way to Me is through much suffering. The way to help your brothers is through suffering. I ask you to suffer this day with joy. Only in My Heart will you experience the love you need to suffer with joy. Come to Me and come to My Heart. Find your peace and joy there. Do not run to the world. Run to My arms and rest in My Heart!

I love you so. I am the Sacred Heart of Jesus.

June 12, 1994
Live to Draw Souls To Me

My sweet one, you cannot be attached to the persecution or the glory. Your life cannot be determined by the world. You must be forever consistent in My love. The world will love you and then will hate you. You are a beloved child of My Father. You are deeply loved by God, Father, Son and Holy Spirit, and you are mothered by My very own mother. You, child, are loved unconditionally. You come to My Heart, you find refuge from all you suffer, you are filled with My love.

A heart fixed on Jesus is joyful in suffering. Do not complain to your brothers. Carry your crosses for the sake of souls. Talk to others about the love of God. Have a smile on your face. Reflect the God inside of you. How, child, are you? Are you an open book? Come to My Heart and be filled with My love. You will have an endless supply of love to give to your brothers.

I am the Sacred Heart of Jesus. I am your refuge. I am your might. I am your love. I wait for you to come to Me.

You suffer not in vain. You suffer for your brothers. Live to draw souls to Me. Be so in love with Me that nothing matters but to promote the love of God. Oh, dear ones, time is so short! Your brothers need you to pray for them. Make sacrifices for souls. Your life is so short! Your time here is but a breath. Spend this life serving Me. You, child, are My hands. You are Me to your brothers.

Come to My Heart. Be in union with Me constantly. I love you so, sweet ones. Oh, if you only knew, you would never be down or lose faith. My Heart is a furnace on fire for love of you. Come to Me and I will warm your hearts in Mine and you will warm the cold world. Light up this world with the fire of My love. Come, come, to My Heart!

I love you. Jesus.

The Lamb, Jesus Christ

R.He is the Lamb. The Father loved us so much He gave His own Son that we might have eternal life. Jesus paid the price of our salvation with His Blood. I see Him accepting all silently, to His death, His head bowed down in quiet acceptance, as a little lamb, not noisy, just complying with the Will of the Father.

He is the unbloody sacrifice in the Mass. He complies totally with the Will of the Father, in silence, with such love for us. This is the gift of the Mass. He gives us His own Body in the Eucharist, out of ardent love for us. He gives us Himself. He wants our love. He wants us to be united in such love with Him. God-made-man gives us His very own life! How do I receive Him Who gives Himself to sinful me with such love? Am I blind to what is transpiring here? Holy Spirit, open me up to know the truth about God. Give me all Your gifts so I can better share in the life of Christ, given to me in the Mass.

We Have One Life in Christ

R.Our lives cannot be separated. We must be united in Christ. We do not have our lives and then go to church and share in His life. Our lives are to be lived in Christ.

Christ, be ever in my breast, on my lips, in my actions, in my thoughts. What comes from me is Christ, acting through me. As I become one in Christ, He lives in me and it is a might that cannot be contained. He flows from my actions. He speaks with my tongue. The more I am in union with Him, the more He operates from me. There is a oneness. I live in Him, He lives in me. What flows from me is the life of Christ in me. His love flows to those I touch. The ideal is to be united so closely to Him that my life is His life radiating from me. My life is to be lived minute by minute in union with Him. To put on Christ and to live in this world with His life within me, this is my goal, Christ's life ever present in all my actions.

I Reflect the God Who Lives Within

R.He wants us to put on Christ. All of our actions, our speech, our clothing, how we spend our time, reflect how we preach His gospel. There is not one minute of one day that I am separate from Jesus. My life must be a reflection of Him, totally within me. I cannot wear luring clothes and be Christ to this world. I cannot speak with foul talk and be angry and be Christ to this world. I am the reflection of the God Who lives within me. My every word, action, being must reflect His life within me. I cannot be in union with Him and be separate from Him in some things. I must put on Christ, reflect His being as He lives in me and I live in Him, as I am. I live in this world to preach the gospel of the Lord, Jesus Christ.

The Carpenter

You are he who goes to a carpenter to learn to make a cabinet. You know nothing. You do not have any idea of what you are to do. The carpenter knows exactly. He has a procedure whereby his plan will be accomplished. Every detail must be observed. He is the Master. You do not have the talent. You need talent to do woodwork. If you were given the talent and the directions, you could accomplish this task with such beauty.

I am the carpenter. You are he who needs to be taught. You lack the talent. You need the gifts of the Spirit to accomplish My task! You come to Me in total ignorance. You are open, the Spirit fills you with the gifts. You have everything you need to do My work. The Father created you to accomplish His tasks. You are perfect. You must come open. You must know the plan. The plan is His Will for you. If you do not follow the plan, the cabinet will not be built correctly.

I am the Master. I guide you. I love you. I give you all you need. I walk you through every move. If you try on your own, you have a problem. You know not the way to build cabinets. You know not the way to Me on your own. You must come to Me to be taught. To go it alone is to your own detriment.

Oh, little one, it is so simple. You, in your will, want to work your own plans. You know not how to do it. Only I can teach you what you need to know. Oh, please come to Me. I have all you need. The Spirit fills you with the gifts to know, love and serve God. To go it alone is like trying to build the cabinet with no knowledge of woodworking. Oh, little ones, I love you. Come to Me. Let Me teach you. The Will of the Father is the happiness for your life.

I am Jesus Christ, Son of God. I am God. I, God, long to be with you and teach you. Go not off on your own. Come to Me. I love you so!

June 13, 1994
The Way to Love Is to Affix Yourself to My Heart

Love to save souls. Did your brother offend you and say awful things to you? Think of his soul. You are here to help your brothers and love them. Love is not asking in return. Love is giving without demanding anything back. Do you love to get back? Then it isn't love! "But, God, how do I learn this lesson? It is so hard." My dear, little ones, I love you. You come to My Heart, you see as only the Holy Spirit allows you to see. You see your brother in his suffering and his soul.

Oh, child, does it matter when you think of his soul? Is it such a small act for Me to ask you to love rather than "tolerate" Him, your brother? He will die some day. If he is in darkness, you are My light shining into his being. Do not think of yourself. Think of his soul. Think of your efforts, your attempts to touch him, sweet one. This is the way to touch him now. Don't think about yourself and how you have been wronged. See his soul before God and love for Me.

Child, this pleases Me so much. Do you not know I gave My life for him? I love him so. You give your life for your hurting brother. You give when you want to think of yourself. The way to Me is to follow Me. I loved those who crucified Me. I thought only of the life to come. I thought of saving their souls.

Follow Me, My sweet and wonderful child. Think of saving souls. My mercy is there for every soul. Preach My love in your actions. Put on Christ. I died to save your soul. I died to save their soul. I died that you might be with Me forever in heaven.

Love mends the fence. Love is giving. Love is My way. You are here to help your brothers get to heaven. Life, child, is so short. You cannot do this alone. You need to come to My Heart and constantly dwell there. You need to let go and let Me love through you. I showed you the way. You must decide to unite your life to Mine in such a way that you never wander from My Heart. Then, sweet one, you will love as I love through you. You will see, where you were blind, things you never saw before. You will see the things of God and you will live!

Why Do I Care?

Why am I here? Why do I care? I am your Lord, child. I lend you your time. You can serve Me or you can squander My time.

Think of Me at every moment. There is no need to fret. I am truly caring for you, child, at every moment. Do not worry, this life is so short. If you thought you had one day to live, would you waste it on such incidental things? You, little one, would be with Me and your family. You need not prove yourself to any man. They have the problem with their doubts. You do not doubt. Come to Me.

Come, come, come, come. All day be with Me. Give Me your heart, a quiet love affair with Me while you are with others and doing My work. I am the Great Lover. I loved you to My death, dear one.

June 14, 1995
ROSARY MEDITATIONS
The Glorious Mysteries

Note: This rosary was prayed in the Sorrowful Mother Chapel at Our Lady of the Holy Spirit Center, Norwood, Ohio.

The Resurrection of Jesus

1. *Song:* This is the day the Lord has made. Let us rejoice and be glad. This is the day the Lord has made. Let us rejoice and be glad.
2. ✟ Let go and surrender. Come to Me. I rose on the third day. So, too, you shall rise from all your difficulties and trials. I am Jesus Christ, Son of God. I am present to you, My beloved ones, and I speak to you through this rosary.
3. ✟ Tied to the pillar! Bound to the cross! Are you bound to the difficulties of this life? Let go! Come to Me! Let Me saturate you with My life and you will be raised to such heights as you are lifted high through My life, through My grace. Let go! Surrender and trust! I am the Almighty God. I am within you. Your every thought, your every action you do with Me, My beloved ones, joined in union with Me so that your every thought is a thought

you share with the Almighty God. Do not fear, do not fret. I was victorious and rose from the dead and you, too, if you are joined in union with Me, shall rise victorious from your struggles.

4. ✠ Satan presses down on each one. Each soul he wants to devour, to torment. I am the Almighty God. It is through the Holy Spirit that you are lifted high. Let Me fill your hearts, My beloved ones. Let the Holy Spirit infiltrate your being and you, too, will be raised to such heights, for the Almighty God is a power that cannot be contained. You will feel a releasing of this vibrancy within your being and you will know life as you have never known life before. I am Jesus and I fill you with My life within your very being.

5. ✠ You will experience freedom, for to know Me is to be free of fear. If you realized that the Almighty God lives within you and performs each and every action with you, you are freed from fear.

6. ✠ Great insights into My mysteries I give to you. Many live but are dead in spirit. I impart to you the gifts of the Spirit, the vibrancy of His life radiating within you, filling you and carrying you on your way. You will radiate to all those with whom you come in contact for I am the Almighty God and I live within you and I operate through you to those you touch. Let go! Surrender! Let go of anything that holds you bound. Do not be held bound to your thoughts. Focus on Me.

7. ✠ Do you feel My life as it fills your soul, My dear ones? Let go! Experience My life within. You share in My divine life. Your human nature is elevated to higher levels as you partake more fully in My life. I am the Almighty God, a force too mighty to be contained, and I speak to you and give you My abundant grace. Open wide and absorb all that I am giving you. Do not fret or fear for I am God!

8. ✠ My plan will unfold at this Center despite all those involved and how they resist and are willful in their ways. It is not up to them to operate this plan. This is the plan of the Father. Only in compliance with His Will will His plan work smoothly. It is their own willfulness that is causing this confusion and doubt. I cry out to you to come to Me and be filled with My life for you will be a pillar of strength. As others fumble about you, you will be steadfast in My love and My strength. I am the Almighty God. You I have chosen to hear these words. You are being guarded. Release yourself. Comply with the Will of the Father. The plan will unfold and you are a big part of this plan.

9. ✠ Come unto Me, you who are heavily burdened, and I will give you rest. Release yourselves. The anxiety that you feel within is

quieted and you rest quietly and securely in the arms of the Almighty God.

10. *Song:* New life! New life! You came to bring us new life!

   Song between decades: Come, Holy Spirit, fill our hearts. Enkindle in us the fire of Your love. Come, Holy Spirit, fill our hearts. Enkindle in us, the fire of Your love.

The Ascension

1. ✠ I am the Bread of Life. I give you My life. You are filled, My dear ones, with the life of the Almighty God. Come to Me in the Eucharist for I give you Myself. You will be with all mankind when you unite with Me in the Eucharist. It is through the Holy Sacrifice of the Mass that men will be united in this world. Pray always in union with the Holy Sacrifice of the Mass and feel this union in your spirit with all in the world. To unite with Me is to unite with one another. You cannot be one in Me and be at odds with your brother. To be one in Me is to be in union with all others.

2. **R.** He ascended into heaven! If we envision this sight, the Almighty God going into the sky, we can realize a little of His might.

3. **R.** We see with limited vision. We do not see as we should see. Only through the Holy Spirit, when He opens up our eyes and our ears and our hearts and imparts to us His gifts, will we see more clearly.

   ✠ I give to you, My dear, sweet ones, such insights into the problems in this world. Come to Me and I will fill you with My life and you will understand and comprehend mysteries that others do not see. I am the Almighty God. It is through Me that you will understand more fully this divine plan as it unfolds right before your eyes, for it is My might living in you that will help this plan to unfold as it should. You must come to Me and unite closely. I will operate through you and work in you and minister to all those you touch. I am Jesus, the Almighty God, one, true, magnificent! I am God!

4. ✠ Come unto Me, all who are weary, and you will be lifted to heights you would not dream possible. I apply My grace and you feel the freedom, the freedom of flying. I give to you, My beloved ones, My life within you. You are powered to such heights. Let go of those things that keep you bolted to the ground. Let go of all! Surrender and let Me run your life. Have no judgments toward any man. See him as a creation of the

Father, uniquely created with specialness and dignity. Love all. Look at each person in that person's uniqueness. Look at each person with eyes to see the beauty with which the Father created him or her. Even when in apparent wretchedness, the beauty of the Almighty Creator shines through each soul. It is not up to you to judge, but to love. I give to you this commandment: love God and love one another. In all things love and live according to the Father's Will. It is this by which you will be judged: how you complied with His Will, how you loved one another, all acts performed in greatest love. I am the Almighty God and I give to you this commandment: love God and love your neighbor as yourself.

5. ✠ In the Eucharist, My dear ones, I give you Myself! Do you see that the Almighty God comes to you, inside of you, with such great love? Why do you worry what others say and think? You must love them. Many are hurting this day. Have you loved? Will you love for Me? Will you unite with Me and become one in Me and let Me love from your being? I call you to love. Love, love, love! Always love! Do not let Satan talk in your heads, My dear ones. Do not listen to words that cause division with any man. Come to Me and I will fill you with My divine love.

6. ✠ I will be with you forever and ever and ever. What have you to fear? Your job is to stay focused on Me, to remain in Me and with Me, to live as one in Me. My dear ones, do not be caught up in Satan's crafts, for he is the great deceiver. I give you this commandment: love God and love one another.

7. ✠ I want this rosary to be in the third Blue Book.

8. ✠ I give you, My dear ones, twenty-four hours in each day. Do you have time, time for the Almighty God Who remains on earth with you, no less present than the day that I walked on this earth? Are you too busy for God when I command you to love Me with your whole heart, your whole soul and your whole being? Do you, in your willfulness, go about your way and say, "I am too busy. I will give to you, God, as I feel I can?" I tell you, you are to love God with your whole heart, your whole soul and your whole being and give to Him first. Then all else will work. Man has made other things his gods. I am the Almighty God! There is one God! It is only in living according to the Father's Will that you will have peace and joy in your hearts. Let go, surrender, and you will be raised to such heights in My love.

9. ✠ I fill your souls with My life when you come to Me in the Eucharist and sit in front of the tabernacle. You are raised and elevated to wondrous heights in this life. As the hot air balloon

3. **R.** We consecrate ourselves, our whole beings, to the Hearts of Jesus and Mary.

4. **R.** The Hearts of greatest love: her Heart pierced with a sword, His Heart pierced with a lance, Hearts filled with immense love for all men.

5. **R.** See Mary as the angel comes to her and asks her to be the Mother of God. In compliance with the Father's Will, she says, "Thy Will be Done." All through the lives of Jesus and Mary we see the reflection of Their compliance with His Will. Surrender and love, peace and joy! Mary—her Heart was pierced with a sword. Jesus—His Heart was pierced with a lance. To His death on the cross, He complied with the Father's Will, always in peace. Mary is now crowned with a golden crown, the glory of all heaven and earth! Queen! Queen of heaven and earth! The Father has a plan for each one of us. When we were born, He gave us talents to carry out this plan, each talent given in greatest love for us: the gift to sing, the gift to speak, the gift to write. All of these gifts were handpicked by the Father so that we could carry out His plan, so that we could carry on the work that Jesus had begun on this earth. It is in accordance with this plan that our peace and joy lie and we, too, will be crowned with a crown of glory in heaven. Jesus ascended into heaven to prepare a place for us. Our greatest fear is to be separated from God. This is our only fear. To live in Him is to live! There is no need to fear if we are living in Him.

6. *Song:* Eye has not seen, ear has not heard, what God has ready for those who love Him. Spirit of love, come give us the mind of Jesus. Teach us the wisdom of God.

✚ I give you a new commandment: love one another as I have loved you.

7. **R.** The heavens are opened and man goes to his final destination, all of the tears and worries of this earth left behind. He sees before him the glories of heaven. The kingdom of God is at hand and it is within. My dear ones, open wide your hearts and let Me penetrate deeply. Let Me fill you with My love and you will know that the kingdom of God lives within.

8. ✚ I give you the beautiful trees, the birds of the air. I give you far greater gifts, My dear ones. Many look at this world with dark colored glasses. I give you My life! Open up your eyes and pray for vision to see those gifts I am giving to you this day. Let your hearts be filled with joy, for I live! I live in this world this day! I never abandon you! Father, Son and Holy Spirit live with-

in your heart when you are in the state of grace. What have you to fear when the Almighty God lives within you. Alleluia. Alleluia. Alleluia. Their eyes were opened and their tongues were loosed and they proceeded throughout their lives, forever declaring the works of the Lord. Alleluia.

9. ✠ I give to you the gift of your tongue, the tongue upon which you receive the Almighty God. My dear ones, use your tongue to sing the praise of the Almighty God Who comes and is received on this tongue. If I come to you on your tongue, how can you with your tongue, sin? My dear ones, guard your tongue as the entryway to your soul. As a man is in his heart, so shall he be to this world. I give you a new commandment: love God with your whole heart, your whole soul and your whole being, and love your neighbor as yourself. Do not speak harshly against your brother. Do not talk about your brothers for they were created by My Father and redeemed by My Blood. They are precious to Me. Who are you that you can judge these little ones? Judging is not up to you. Loving is what you are commanded to do.

10. ✠ I am the Sacred Heart, on fire for love of men. I came to this earth, suffered, died and rose on the third day to bring you life. The kingdom of God is within you, My dear ones. Guard your tongue. May your hearts be ever pure. May your hearts be filled with love. May you silence Satan in your heads for he aims to trip you and rob you of your joy. Satan wants to take the life from within you. Let go, surrender and trust for you are guarded far more than the finest pearls. You are watched and protected by the Almighty God Who lives in this world this day.

Song: Come unto Me, all who are weary, and find rest in your soul. Come unto Me, all who are burdened. I will comfort thee.

✠ Love one another as I have loved you.

Song after the last decade: Praise God from Whom all blessings flow. Praise Him all creatures here below. Praise Him above ye Heavenly Hosts. Praise Father, Son and Holy Ghost. Amen.

June 15, 1994

Your Direction Comes from God and God Alone

Dear little, scared ones, do not fret. Do you not know I never leave you? You worry, you are afraid. I am guarding you. Think of a blind man coming down the street. He may walk in front of cars and lose his life. What is to become of him if he continues to walk around blindly and do as he pleases?

(I had a vision of many cars parked on the street but not moving).

Many of My children are blind and in darkness. They continue to walk around and do as they please. Is it fair that they do this? Every man has a free will. The blind man can take precautions and he will not be harmed. He can't do as he pleases. He is blind.

You are blind men. You can't do as you please. You must get the direction of one who will lead you safely to your destination. Pray to the Holy Spirit to open your eyes to the truth. This world is full of falsities. Well-intentioned children are falling into disaster because they wander aimlessly around, like the blind man, with no direction.

Your direction comes from God and God alone. Come and sit with Me in front of My tabernacle. Oh, I love you so much, My little ones. Do not worry. I will take good care of you.

Pray and let go of your anxiety. I never leave you. Believe Me, I am truly by your side guarding you. I love you.

June 16, 1994   3:15a.m.

I Am by Your Side Always

My little one, be of a clean heart. When you are weary, come to My Heart. I am Jesus, Son of the Living God. I talk in your head. You see Me, you know I am here. Fear not for I will sustain you.

Life here is so short. You must focus only on My love. I truly talk to you. You have nothing to fear. In the days that follow, no matter how difficult, I will be by your side. You must have faith in Me and My work for you.

Your job is to promote My ardent love. Never lose sight of the fact that souls will be saved by your efforts to do this. This is no little matter. The devil constantly will try, in these days, to trip you up. You will be tested to stay steadfast in My love.

I do not want to upset you, only to warn you and tell you that souls are at stake. My letters will turn men's hearts to Me. You must constantly focus on My love for you. Circulate your letters. They are so vital to turning men to the love of God.

Soon your burden will be lifted and you will feel some relief. You must be in constant prayer. Being with your children is a prayer for you. Come to the Center. You feel Real Presence there. I will give you miracles there. Pray in the chapel with your children. They will become closer to Me through prayers as you spend time playing with them. You need simplicity in your life. Live only for love of Me.

(I see little white lights on my notebook).

In Your Suffering, Become Intimate with Me

Ed. Note: The following occurred during the praying of a rosary at home.

R.(Agony). You, Jesus, did not lose Your focus on the Father, and You still had peace in Your Heart, but You sweat blood, so I think about my mental anguish. Such anguish, to sweat blood! Do You know mental anguish? You were a human and You knew You were going to die this brutal death. How I anguish over doing what You tell me to do. How ashamed I feel when You ask so little!

(Scourging). They beat Me. I held nothing back. They tore My beloved flesh. I bled. They took My body, tied Me to a pole and beat Me. I could not move. I was bound. I give you freedom to choose to do little things and you say no. I could have broken the cords, I was God. I stayed bound, and subject to this awful violation of Me, for love of you. I love you. Don't ever say no to little acts I ask you to do to prove your love for Me. This offends Me so! I gave so much for you, little one. The acts I ask you to do are for your own good.

Accept suffering, accept it as your life with Me. I ask you to suffer. You miss My lessons I so sweetly teach. Quit complaining, suffer in silence, suffer with joy. Love your children, do not be glum around them. I call you to hard tasks. Do the hard things. Watch the results! Strive to be a saint. Saints never complain. Suffer My scourging by joyful acceptance of suffering. It is My way. It will save souls!

R.His Passion has meaning in how He suffered. How little He asks of us, yet we cannot even do it!

(Carrying of the Cross). Their eyes met, both in acceptance, both suffering, both silent, both knowing they had to accept it and He could stop it at any moment. He did it totally. They wept inside. How do we weep when we are offended? Did they holler from the housetops or weep softly? With such pain inside, her Heart pierced with such sorrow, as she beheld her beloved Son! Both weeping in silent surrender in such brutality.

Is this a lesson in silence? Silent acceptance! This is my lesson. I am complaining. Where am I? Certainly not a light that shines in the darkness! Doing His Will is silent acceptance. "She did it, He did it? It is so hard." How blind we are to so much!

(Crucifixion). She stood under the cross and cried to herself. Silent acceptance. She didn't protest.

How the body wants all to know how we suffer. Take away

the pain. Did she take pain medicine or did He? They accepted in silence this horror. And We complain and complain!

Suffer, My child, with joy. This is a key to sainthood. Pull your phones from the walls and take your complaints to My Heart. You are missing such rewards and I have to give you more suffering to learn the lesson.

R.Sweet surrender! It is as if I have a secret with Jesus and it binds me to Him. It is hard, but then I feel such unity with Him. He and I know, as Mary and Jesus felt when they looked into each other's eyes, such oneness to share the suffering. Such oneness, to share My intimate suffering with Jesus alone! What a treasure I lose, to miss such an intimate connection with Jesus! We have a secret. This creates such intimacy! He knows my heart. I mature in My relationship with Him.

Intimacy is sharing with the exclusion of others. To be intimate with Him, I share things with Him and not others. Suffering is such intimacy!

To suffer and carry it and be glum casts a shadow on your fellows. To suffer and share only with Me creates a love, a bond and a trust that cements our hearts together.

R.The deepest suffering was shared between Jesus and Mary, looking at each other in total silence. Silence is the key to receiving benefits from suffering. "Suffer for Me with joy! Receive such a reward!"

Do you wear your problems on your chest? "Oh," you say, "I have so much to learn and I fail so miserably," and I say you are blind and you must come to Me to be taught! Suffer with joy and in silence!

R.He is showing us constantly how we can have a deeper union with Him. It is I who keep myself away from Him.

Suffering is a bearing down. When you suffer, there is a weight you carry on your back. He asks us to suffer, to carry this cross with joy. As He carried His cross, He asks us to carry ours with greatest joy.

June 16, 1994
Suffer with Jesus and Mary

Look, child, at Us as We suffer all through this Passion. Quiet acceptance, a sharing in our eyes meeting! I ask you to suffer in silence. Carry your cross. Do not give your burdens to others. You are this light that shines in the darkened world. If I give you sufferings and you complain, your light does not shine.

You can accept your cross or reject it. If you accept your cross, you should carry it, not give the burden to others. This is sainthood. This develops intimacy with Me and our eyes meet and we know the suffering, as the suffering between My mother and Me!

The way to Me is to pick up your cross and follow Me as I trod in silent surrender.

R. Their eyes meeting is the key. This is how our eyes meet with theirs. This is intimacy. This is union in their Hearts. His Heart was lanced, her Heart was pierced.

Bring your suffering to Our Hearts and be united to Us. In suffering there is pain, sometimes physical pain, sometimes pain in the heart. There is a bearing down with pain, the carrying of a load.

R. If He went out in such suffering, why do we think we should not have to suffer?

Life is a bittersweet symphony, My child. You have a mixture of suffering and pleasure. The way to Me is the cross, to relinquish your life here and live it totally for Me.

Suffering suffered for Me lasts forever. It is the crown I wore that won your salvation. It is in your suffering you will help to save souls.

You are not here for momentary pleasures. I ask you to carry crosses, to carry the burdens that I place on you. It is through these burdens you are drawn closer to Me.

Accept your suffering with joy. It is in this joy that you will find the true joy of everlasting happiness.

I love you so. I am your Jesus and I will make more teachings clear to you in your life. Live My Passion with Me and come closer to the Hearts of Me and My mother.

June 16, 1994

He Asks Us to Fast

R. Pleasure and pain. Animals seek pleasure. They want to eat and be satisfied. We are created in the image of God to understand so much more than momentary pleasure.

See their eyes meet. His Heart was lanced, her Heart was pierced. Sorrow between them was so intense, more so than joy between two people. There is unity in that gaze between them, a joining. There is a unity with us when we join our hearts to their Hearts in quiet acceptance of all that they send us, whether it be pain or joy. They ponder the ways of our hearts. They know the true hearts that beat within us.

Such sorrow, such joy, joy to be united, sorrow to suffer the pain. It is in sweet surrender you are joined to Our Hearts. You accept all I have given you, you consecrate yourselves to our hearts, a total surrender of yourself to the Hearts of Mary and Jesus.

R. The gaze between them is enough to write volumes. The suffering that exists between them! How tenderly she had looked upon her infant baby and then beheld His lifeless body on her lap after He was taken down from the cross!

Union between the Two Hearts of mother and Son, union between our hearts and Theirs. It is in being detached regarding the things of this world that we are joined with them. Total consecration to Their Hearts, our hearts merging with Theirs in total fusion! It is in this oneness that I can put on Christ and preach the gospel in my very being, to be joined as one with Mary and Jesus!

June 16, 1994
Study Christ to Become Christ-like

R. It is in studying Christ that I learn to be Christ-like. Christ says to study His Passion. It is there He teaches us true love, to lay down our lives for our friends.

To understand His love, I must study how He loved. He loved in silent surrender. He and Our Blessed Lady both suffered such anguish silently and willingly. They did not complain, they did not cry out in pain.

He is here today. He gives Himself to us in Holy Communion. He is totally present. He gives me the cross. I carry it a while, then I want to give it back. Carry it until the end! Suffering leads to union with God. If I search for that which the soul craves in anything worldly, it is a futile search.

God alone knows our hearts so well. No human can fully understand our suffering. God fully knows us from when we were born. No human can give us the compassion, love, and understanding as He, since He knows us so well. He knows us far better than we know ourselves. We turn to Him. He knows we don't have to explain.

As Jesus looked at Mary, they didn't have to say a word. To turn to Jesus in suffering, we don't have to say a word. He knows our hearts far better than we. We look, He knows. No human being can share this with us. This creates union.

Suffer with Joy

I ask you to suffer with joy, child. Take the cup of suffering. Accept it. My way is the way of the cross. Suffer with Me as I ask you to suffer. I love you. I never give you more than you can handle. Know that My Will for you is to suffer with joy.

A prophet is without honor in his own town. Stay steadfast in Me and accept what I give you. It comes with greatest love. Have nothing but peace in your heart. The world may hate you one minute and love you the next minute. Remain in Me. I am there. I am consistently in love with you. I am all that you are absolutely sure of. I will never abandon you. I will never give you more than you can handle. Surrender your hearts to Me and to My mother. Give yourself entirely to Me and I will sustain you. I love you so, My precious ones.

These Messages Are Mine

My child, do not worry, fret or fume. I am handling My messages. They are Mine. They will see as never before that I am God and I am truly speaking to you here. I want My Will obeyed. I will see to the publishing of these messages. I cried bloody tears because of My sorrow to be ignored.

I am God. I am speaking. Time in short. Souls will be lost because they do not know the love of God. I am God. All that matters is that My beloved ones get to heaven. Some of My people, My children, will lose their souls. This is the mighty medicine: I want My letters to circulate. I want My letters published. Why has My letter for Falmouth been held up? There are many souls that will suffer because of these delays. Nothing will draw a soul to heaven except My love. I am writing personal love letters to all My children. I want My messages published. I am your Jesus. I cry blood to see My children lose their souls. Do you know how this world is hurting?

Do you know how many will be condemned to eternal hell? Do you realize what this world is doing to children? Little children will never even know of My love. Their parents are teaching them sick lessons. I want My letters of love for each soul published. I love every soul. I am so wounded. I bled for their souls. They will go to eternal damnation. Nothing here is of any account unless it draws you toward heaven. This world is so sick.

You hold the mighty medicine. They need this medicine to turn their hearts to Me. Please circulate My letters. Please, please. Some of My beloved ones will burn forever. It is so sad, the sin in this world. It is so sad, this world full of decay. I give you My personal love letters for My beloved ones and you hold them up for fear. I love My beloved children. Nothing matters here unless it promotes My love and love for each other.

My letters talk about My on-fire love for each soul. Please, I am Jesus Christ, the Son of God. I am talking to you all and beg you to listen to Me this day. Souls are at stake. Some of My children will never know My love. I profess My love here. Please. I love you so much. It is love for which you live, love of God, love of one another. Nothing else matters. This world is sick. They need these messages. I tell you all you need to know. Read My messages. I am God. I am speaking here. I beg you. I love you. This is an urgent plea to take Me seriously. Jesus.

June 18, 1994
His Burning Love

R. His love is burning, enkindling. He says, "My Heart burns for love of you." Such emotion, to have the thought of His Sacred Heart burning for us, and He is asking us to come and dwell in such ardent love!

Come, child, through the pure heart of My beautiful mother. She will take you to the deepest part of My Heart and you will dwell with Me in such deep love. This is real love, given from God, God Who is the root of all love, an on-fire, burning love of Him Who longs for each soul.

R. To behold the Sacred Heart of Jesus, to see the Heart, as I did once, as an open furnace and to have Mary place us in the furnace of His love. Such seclusion, tucked away in the recesses of His Heart!

My love is enkindling, burning, smoldering. It burns deeply for you, My beloved. Feel the emotion of this most tender love, given just for you.

R. I want to know this burning Heart of Jesus, on fire for love of little me. Then I look at the crucifix above the tabernacle, life-size, and I see that You truly have this love. This is the love that led You to give Your own precious life for me.

My God, I am on fire for love of You. Such intimacy with God! I love You so! You are truly here and in my breast now after Communion. Oh, Lord, I am in awe for love of You!

A Verse of Love

R. You were created by God the Father out of such love. You are His divine creation. He loves you this very day.

You were loved, before you were born, with such love. The love given all the humans that ever lived, could not compare with God's love for you.

Jesus is alive and waits for you in the Eucharist. He is present, Body, Blood, Soul and Divinity, the same as the day He died.

The Holy Spirit is the love between the Father and the Son. The Holy Spirit has gifts for you: knowledge, from God; wisdom, from God; fortitude for strength, and understanding from God, counsel, from God himself, fear of God and piety to be holy.

You are so loved! You are perfectly created by the Father. You are God's gift to this world. You have dignity because God created you. You are so precious to Him. You are His beloved one.

Jesus loves you with such an ardent, on-fire love. It is burning for you. He awaits you in the tabernacle. Go to Him and share His love! He wants to be so close to you!

I am Jesus Christ, the Son of God. I love you, I love you, I love you. Read My letters given to each of you personally. I want you to know of My ardent love. Come to Me and let Me fill you with love, love from God! Open this book anywhere and I will speak to you. I love you.

R. Jesus loves you so much He would die for you alone today. He shed His blood for you.

I Ask You to Love Me More Than Yourself

Dear one, what I ask you to do is not what you want to do many times. You do it because you love Me more than yourself. Yes, dear one, I ask you to love Me more than you love yourself. Will you do that for Me? Ask for help to know more about love. I am Love. As I teach you, you learn a little more. If you love Me more than yourself, you will do many things that were once hard.

Total surrender is what I expect of you. When you see any abuse of the Eucharist, speak out. Child, you know how I am present, how I talk to you. I am in the Eucharist, every particle, Body, Blood, Soul and Divinity. Such irreverence by those who take Me to the sick. People need to know how truly present I am in every particle. This is God. They treat Me so irreverently.

Trust Me, sweet one. I will be your guide. Pray the Prayer for Union with Me. I ask for a total giving of yourself. You hold nothing back. You do not worry about what others think, you love Me first, above all things. Trust Me. Do you not know I calmed the storm? You must never doubt Me and My presence with you. My sweet and adorable child, totally surrender to Me. I am your beloved. I love you so. I am Jesus. I am the Son of God and I love you.

R.What do you think would pay the price for all the sins of mankind and win their eternal life in heaven? It must be the Father loved us so much, but He is just. Look at all the sins for all mankind - look at all the reward of everlasting happiness. The greatest sacrifice the Father could give was the gift of His only Son! He loves us this much!

He loved us this much. He is so just. The priest said, "Why does God allow awful things to happen to good people?" We do not know the ways of the divine God. We humans cannot ever understand, on earth, His ways. He is divine. We are human. He reveals some understanding to us as He draws us closer to the one, triune God.

Oh, Mary, let me love God through you. Such closeness, through your pure and loving Heart, such intimate union with Him, my one, true God!

Feel the Warmth of the Love of God and My Mother

My Heart is burning, burning, burning for you. Tell them how much I want to enkindle such love deep, deep in My Heart. Go to Mary. Ask her to place you securely in My Heart.

I am the Lord, Jesus Christ. I am the Son of God. I am Who am and your life is opening more to greater intimacy with Me. Focus on the furnace of My love. Focus on its intensity, deep within My Heart. My Heart is burning, child. You must constantly think of this intense love given for you.

I love You so much, My sweet one! Tell them about this love I have for each and every soul! Focus on the furnace of My love. Go to Mary, My mother. Oh, she loves you each so! You are so loved by My Father and the Holy Spirit!

Feel this warmth of the love of God deep, deep in your heart. We are truly present. We dwell in you after Communion. Such a gift, My little, precious one. This is the gift of God, given to you.

Oh, child, feel the intensity of this love poured out to you in the Holy Eucharist.

I am Jesus Christ, the Son of God. I dwell in your heart.Such honor, honor for you, My beloved. Come and be bathed in the precious love of God, Father, Son and Holy Spirit. Be drawn into My Heart with the deep love of My mother. Oh, child, read this again and again. My Heart burns for love of you. I love you. Jesus.

You Were Blind, But Now You See

Oh, little blind one, do you now see? I will take care of My messages. You will speak as I said you would. Do you think I am teaching you this for no reason? You will sing My messages. I give you emotion, I cry out to you. Do not fear. Anyone who reads one message knows you do not know this material. I am simple. I am direct. I am profound.

I am God, child. I talk to you. Do you believe Me? I am Jesus Christ, Son of God. You will preach My words for Me. Concentrate on your intimacy with Me. I wanted you here. Let each moment unfold.

Dear one, I am in control of your life. Let go entirely. Surrender totally to Me. I am God. I am your beloved, loving, loving Jesus. Oh, dear one, tell My dear ones of this love—burning, smoldering, intense, ardent. Oh, sweet one, do not hold back. You have the messages to help so many be drawn to My most Sacred Heart. They need this message. I have entrusted it to you. I ask this of you this day, that you speak from your heart to every soul you meet. I will guide you. Love for Me, child. Do not hold back! You were blind, now you see. Pray to the Holy Spirit, My beloved ones. Souls are at stake and time is, oh, so short! Oh, beloved, I intently love you and long to be united to your heart. Come to Me and be so close to Me here. I love you. I love you. I love you.

(I saw rays off the moon, long ones, a double moon. One night in the big chapel I saw the same rays off all the candles.)

Love Casts Out Fear

R.I don't care if I see with my eyes. I care if I see You. To know You, to know You in my heart. Where I was blind, I now see. Do I see You, Who so sweetly teach me each day with such love? Do I see You and know You are truly there whether I see You with eyes or with my heart?

Open up the gates to your heart, child, and there experience the one, true, magnificent God. Open your heart and feel His burning love for you, sweet one. In the very recesses of My Heart you will find such refuge. I come to you and I dwell in your heart deeply, truly present and forever with you. Where you wander do not go ever from Me. My Heart is forever with you.

I am God. I can do all things. You do not understand such unity in your heart. You only know more and more how it truly exists. Our hearts are united as one. Your life reflects the actions of the one, true God Who is truly present within your breast. I am the Sacred Heart of Jesus. I want to dwell inside of you in such union, 24 hours a day. Feel My burning love within your very breast. I burn for ardent love of you. My mother unites with Me in your love for Me. She places you deeply in My Heart. We are one with each other in Our Hearts. Think of this union with Me. This will keep you holy. To be so closely united, you will never want to offend Me.

Writing letters about your union with Me is more important than many other letters. I want an intimate, on-fire love relationship with each soul. My Heart is a burning fire. It is an abyss of fervent love, a furnace on fire for the love of you. You do not understand. You must pray to be drawn closer and closer to My Heart. This is your refuge. This is your strength. This is what will give you the drive to do this work I ask of you. You are to promote My on-fire, ardent love and devotion to the Two Hearts. You are to emphasize the love of God and, thus it follows, love for one another. You are to lead many to Our Hearts. I am Jesus. I never leave you orphaned!

I come to set this world on fire with My love. I died a brutal death for all. I come to tell them now of this love. My Passion and suffering, and that of My mother, are the keys to knowing such love. I remain this day in all the tabernacles of this world with such love for all My beloved ones. I come and give you Myself in the Eucharist. This is the closest union with Me. You must preach the Real Presence. It is in the Eucharist that you will understand My burning love for you. My Heart is burning, on fire for love of My beloved ones. I love them so. This I ask of you. The more you love Me, the more intimate you become with Me, the more you will light up this world with the fire of My love. Love casts out fear! Focus on My love for you and your fear will dwindle. You will live for Me. Consecrate your hearts to Me and My beautiful mother. We love you so!

Pray to Know the Truth

R. Dear Jesus, just as I look at a beautiful tree so ardently sculptured by the hand of God, I submit myself to You and ask You to mold me into Your creative art. I want to operate as You do within me. Come, Lord, please possess my soul and work from my being. I want to live to draw souls close to You. I want to live for Your love.

I am not perfect, Lord. When I think I am perfect or I think I should be perfect, I have a problem. It is in the truth that I am set free. I make mistakes and I am sorry, because I offend You and offend others. Help me, Lord, to see the truth. Holy Spirit, open my eyes and heart to the blindness I have and help me to see more and more what I need to see to please You.

I am Yours, Jesus. I consecrate myself to the hearts of Jesus and Mary and ask for help to answer Your call.

Little one, little one, you indeed are not perfect, but in your faults I still love you. Pray to know the truth. Pray to please Me. Pray for My strength. I am always with you. Focus on Me, intimately united to you at every moment in your heart. Satan constantly wants you to focus on your faults or promote your ego. Live only to love and serve Me. Live to draw others to heaven.

I am your God. I am your Jesus. I am with you. Let go.

Try to live only to serve Me. Pray that you live to spread My love. Live by truth. Satan wants to deceive you. Be not swallowed up by him.

Promote My Love

Dear child, this is the message. Let Me write to you and teach you this lesson for all My people.

Time is so short and I must tell you to reach as many souls as possible. Do not give in to Satan in any way to stop you. Listen in your heart and do as I tell you in everything. Today is the Age of the Two Hearts. Consecrate yourselves to My Heart and that of My Mother. My Mother is here to lead you to such union with Me. She is calling you to do this work. Do not focus on what you say or don't say. Make yourself selfless and exist for love of Me and to save souls.

I am Jesus Christ, the Son of God. Do as you are instructed and pray, pray to help you in everything. Do not listen to Satan to tell you to hold back.

Promote My love. This is your mission, first and foremost, above all other things you do. Promote My love. Do not explain problems. You will have them. People do not want to relinquish their free wills. You live to promote My love. You love to draw souls to My kingdom. This is your call. Live in Me.

I am Jesus. I have spoken. Amen.

June 22, 1994 After Communion at Holy Spirit Monastery, Conyers   8:00a.m.

Jesus and Mary Are United in Their Hearts

Dear sweet one, when you love Me more than you love yourself, you will operate to serve Me. Put aside the things of this world and focus on that for which you have been created. You have been created to serve Me, sweet little one.

If you hold back and doubt, My words will not get out. This is Satan's target, to focus on you. You must focus on Me and our love for one another. You live for Me, to spread My love and draw souls to heaven.

Do not judge My relationship with you by what the world thinks. You are looking for confirmation in the world that I am truly communicating to you, then you are telling others to know Me in their hearts, but you go to the world!

I will never abandon you though you suffer persecution. I suffer with you. When you are ignored, it is Me they are rejecting. I, Jesus Christ, the Son of God, Who lived and died a brutal death on Calvary, speak to you, My precious, beautiful one. Never doubt Me again.

Trust in Me. Go to Me. Your relationship is with Me. I am God. I will sustain you. Go to Me and talk to Me. Tell Me your heart. I am truly a Person and I truly know your every need. I knew you, sweet one, before you were born. I know all your suffering and joy. I know you far better than you know yourself. Come and dwell in My Heart. Take all your cares to Me and rest there. My mother is united to Me. We will bathe you in such love.

R. Mary and Jesus are united in Their Hearts. The meeting of their eyes on Calvary, the union in suffering! The union is knowing each other's hearts, creating this bond of oneness. Mary places you in the very recesses of her Son's Heart. They are united. Love unites. We are one in Him and He is one in us. Surely Mary is one in Him. He is one in the Father and the Father is one in Him. He is one with the Holy Spirit because He is God and the Holy Spirit is God. We are united as one in our hearts if we are in the state of grace. God dwells within us in our hearts. He says He is one in us, we are one in Him.

I feel this burning in my chest to hear Him say He burns for love of us! He is in me. I am planted in His burning Heart, placed there deeply by Mary. Such union! All day I can experience union with Him instantly if I think how He said He burns for love of us. His Heart is a burning vat. It is a furnace of love. It is our haven from this cold and indifferent world. When they slap your face and show you indifference, go to the recesses of His Heart and be enkindled with fire from His love. You then respond with such love to those who smite you. He loves through you your hurting brothers. He gives to them His ardent love. The fire of His love is alive in you as you find refuge in His most Sacred Heart.

Fill me, wash me, cleanse me, polish me. I am the empty vessel ready to be used for the service of His love. I cannot love as He loves. He must dwell within me in such union.

My heart is ablaze with the fire of His infinite love. It never dies, it does not falter, it is enkindled as only He, in his magnificence, can do.

Fire, child, a raging fire is My love for you! Do you feel burning in your chest? Focus on this intense furnace of My love for you. I burn for love of you. I am the refuge to a cold heart. I come and set it on fire with My love.

You must enkindle in your brothers the love I plant deeply in your heart. You must love when they hate you. I will send a spear of fire into their soul when you touch them with this love of mine that I send through you.

Tolerance, you say? Tolerance for your brother? I call you to such love that you would die for him. This is the love I have for you. Die to yourself. Let My love flow as a mighty brook from your very soul. Let Me fix you so deeply in My Heart. You are a vat of My love, from which flows My ardent love for all. Die, die, die to this self that demands its own way, that wants its rights. This self is keeping you from serving Me. I am calling you to an on-fire, ardent love, and you go to the world for little love. All love has its origins in Me. Come to Me, be filled first-hand and then give it to your brothers. Be an empty vessel that I fill with My love and use to love this hurting world.

Come to My Heart, little one, let Mary place you deeply in My Heart and feel the furnace of My love. Be united to God every minute of every day. Let Me dwell deeply in your heart.

I love you so, My special one, created by the hands of My Father, loved so far beyond your belief! Let Me love you, then give My love to your brothers in this world. This world needs the on-fire love of Jesus Christ. Come and sup with Me and experience My burning love.

R. Love is giving. I want my heart to be clean to hold God in it, to love Him, to give to Him. He gives Himself to us and we give ourselves to Him.

Mary, teach me to love your Son as you did. I do not know how to love God. Mary, you loved the Father, you loved the Son, you loved your Spouse, the Holy Spirit. Teach me to love as you love. Work in my heart to know how to love God more. Jesus, teach me to love Your Mother more!

I know so little of love. I am so blind. Holy Spirit, give me fire to love as You love. I am so naive about all this. I am blind. Where I was blind, let me see more and more Your love and give Your love to my brothers.

Holy Spirit, enlighten me. Father, You gave the greatest gift of love. You gave us your own Son that we might have eternal life. Teach us to love. Please, Father, I implore You that I may love God more and more.

Quit analyzing where you are with your brothers. Live to love. Do not fret. Try only to love and, when you fall, humbly admit your failings and proceed to love.

You are not perfect. To think you are, is to hold on to falsity. You commit sins, you offend your brothers, you offend Me. Live to love and ask to be drawn ever closer to My Heart. Repent of your sins and ask for forgiveness. Forgive your brothers and love them. This is My desire, that you love your brothers as I have loved you, that you lay down your life for your brothers and see the creation of the Father in them. This is My command: love God first and love your brothers as yourself.

June 23, 1994 After Communion at Holy Spirit Monastery, Conyers
Come to the Light

R. (An interior vision:) I see Him being taken down from the cross, a ladder, his body is entirely lifeless, slumped over, no resistance, totally life-like. She watches. Such relief, it is over. Such pain to see Him totally dead, after watching His anguish for three hours. The first touch of His lifeless body on her skin, this child she had held tenderly in her arms, the beloved child she had fed, loved, touched, with life in His body, not totally lifeless, dead. This is her beloved child!

Is this not how her children affect her Heart? We are her beloved children. We are given the life of grace in our hearts at baptism and throw away the graces and commit sins. Many of her children choose darkness over light.

It is this life, child, that I give to you, My life within you. Do you see Us suffer for the children in darkness? As Mary suffered so to see My lifeless body, the beloved child of her womb, she suffers so to see the lifeless souls of her children, dark in sin.

R. Oh, Mary, our mother, pray for us that we may turn from our blind ways and see only the ways of God. Mary suffered so to see the physical, human life go from Christ's body. Think how she suffers to watch the children spiritually dead in their souls, to watch the life of grace leave them.

She is our loving mother. She is always so close to us.

Mary speaks:

My little, dear ones, I watch over you. I am your loving mother. I care for your souls. I want to draw you to my beloved Son and His intense love for you, but you go so far after such things that mean nothing. Oh, children, turn your hearts to Him. He loves you so. We suffer for your indifference to Him. We suffer that you are so willful and do not see. Pray to the Holy Spirit to open your eyes, to give you His gifts. He loves you so, my dear little children. You have a loving Father, a loving mother who watches over you. Do not be willful, little ones. Come to us. Come back to my Son. He is the life in your soul. He loves you ardently. He is ablaze for love of you. Come, children, come to Jesus. Pray, pray, pray, my sweet ones. We love you so. We suffer with your darkness. Come to the light, come to the light of my Son, Jesus Christ. Your souls are at stake, little ones. This world has led many astray. You must pray and sacrifice. I love you. I am your loving mother and thank you for responding to my call.

My Mother Calls You Today

My precious one, put yourself in My presence and be with Me. This is My Holy Hill. You will experience such graces when you come and pray with Me here.

I am Jesus, your precious Savior. I have come to fulfill all the Scriptures. You are in an age of Satan. He has overtaken many men's hearts. They do not even know they are disconnected from

My life. I am so sorry for their souls. this day, please commit yourself totally to talking and sending messages to turn men's hearts to My precious love!

I am the Savior of the world! My mother is calling. She is calling you to this place and to this call to turn men's minds to the intimate love of Me. I am Jesus, Son of God. I am the Savior of the world. I come not to destroy the law and the prophets, but to fulfill it. I ask you to spread your letters. They are My letters of love, hand-delivered to each soul. I ask you to do this with all your heart, to love Me more than you love yourself. I am your Jesus. I am the Savior of the world. It was in My death souls were saved. I paid the price for their salvation by My very own blood, shed for love of them.

All will enter My kingdom who follow My commands. Cast out Satan. He wants to trip you up and make you lose your soul. I am your Savior. I am the Savior of the world. Your ransom is My blood. Come to Me for your life. I give to you abundantly and you will be saved. You will inherit the kingdom of My Father. You will see the face of God and you will live. Come to Me, My beloved ones. I shed My very own blood for you. I love you.

June 25, 1994

Mary, Lead Us to Your Son

R. It is Mary who held her Son so tenderly.
It is Mary who saw it all with her eyes.
It is Mary who held the lifeless body of Christ.
It is Mary, so united to Jesus, who knows Him so well, who will
 lead us to Jesus.
I can't do it on my own. I need Mary.
She wants to lead us to her Son.
Prepare ye a way for her Son.
As she delivered Him, she delivers us to Him now.
With ardent devotion, she gives us to Him now.

Mary speaks:
Behold my Son, I bore for love of you, my child, out of such love, through the Holy Spirit. Through me and the Holy Spirit, He was conceived by the Will of the Father for love, such love for you, my beloved children. You are my very own children, too. I beg you, as your mother, to return to my precious Son. Go to Him, little ones. He loves you so. Go to the Eucharist. Receive and eat His Body and His Blood, given for you. Oh, such love for you. You give yourself with Him to the Father. What a sacrifice of love! Go to Mass, receive Him in the Eucharist, the bread of life.

Jesus speaks:
I give you My body, I give you My blood, I give you My life!

R.I am called by you, Mary, to spread the love of your Son. I answer this call, Mary.

Mary speaks:
I am calling you, I am calling you.

R.She is calling us to the Eucharist, to Jesus. He is here with us now. He gives us His body. He shows us signs. He gave His life, we want more. Where is the faith? He was right in the boat and they thought they would drown. He is right in our midst and it is we who do not see Him in our hearts.

We want it our way, not His way. The lesson we must learn about the True Presence is that we do not see but believe it is truly Jesus. "Where you were blind, you now see. Blessed is he who has not seen and has believed." The way to God is through faith.

One of the lessons of the True Presence is that we believe, but do not see.

June 26, 1994

Mary, Teach Us to Love

R.So many sins we commit are with the tongue, yet Jesus chooses to enter our bodies through our mouth. Who am I that He comes to me and I receive the one, true, God-made man? How much I must do that displeases Him! I do not know how I offend Him with my selfish ways. I do not know that I hurt my brothers. I am blind. I pray to You, Holy Spirit, open my eyes so I can see with Your eyes and love my brothers more and more each day. Jesus, teach me to love. Mary, place me in your Immaculate Heart and help me to love more like Jesus and like you. Father, my beloved Father, You are my God, I love You so! Thank You for creating me in Your own image. Help me to know Your fatherly love. Help me to love You more and more.

Oh, I am a creature! You are God! I want to love You, God, more and more. Help me to know, Mary, how to love my precious God more. Place me in the Heart of Jesus and surround me with your own Immaculate Heart. I do not deserve such love, but I am forever grateful to You, three Persons in one God. Praise You. Worship You. I fill You with such honor and praise from my humble heart. Make my heart humble. Wash away my pride. Cleanse me in my heart with a bath of love, flushing out all impurities. Oh, Jesus, Mary, Joseph, teach me the ways of the heart.

Mary touched so tenderly her infant son. She held Him so close to her body and loved Him. Joseph loved Mary and Jesus so very much.

She held Jesus and mothered Him with such tender love. She also loves us.

Oh, Joseph, you loved Jesus and Mary so. Help me to love them more. I love you, oh, Holy Family. Open my heart to experience the love of such a holy family. Help me to join my heart to the union of mother and Son and Son and mother. Help me to know you, St. Joseph, and your patient love, more.

Our Father Is Love

R.My Father is Love. He is a Father, like no earthly Father. He chose to create me in His own image. He loves me. I am His. I am His divine creation. He is my Father. Mary, help me to love the Father as you did.

The Father's love, to give His only Son in such a brutal sacrifice so that I would have life eternal! He gave His Son so that I may live.

The word "father" has such meaning in this love poured out by our Father on each of us! He fathers us and is ever within us when we are in the state of grace.

My Father. I have a loving Father to care and watch out for me. I am Your little child. You are my Father!

All love that comes from Jesus comes from the Father Who loves us. Jesus is one with the Father, the Father is one with Him and I am one with them and with Mary. We are united in our hearts, one with the Father, Son and Holy Spirit and one with Mary. Through this tender uniting, Jesus is the very center of this union.

I love You so, Jesus. You come to me in the Eucharist, God-made-man, with Your love! Who am I that God enters me and unites with me, a mere mortal? He comes and unites with me in such love for me.

Be ever present and ever one in my heart. Let me live in You and You in me that I may be as You want me to be, totally free and dependent on You for my actions, so that I will be the reflection of God, Father, Son and Holy Spirit, Who live within me.

Mary, help me to love God, Father, Son and Holy Spirit.

You Cannot Straddle the Fence

Nothing here that is worldly matters if it is not rooted in Me. Love one another as I have loved you. I showed you the way. You must follow Me. My way is the way to the Father. My way is the way to eternal life.

Be like Me in all your actions. I came, I showed you the way. You cannot straddle the fence. My way is the only way. It is the way of the cross.

Come to the recesses of My Heart and experience the love of God. Be united with Me and My mother in Our Hearts. Consecrate yourselves to Me, My little ones. Consecrate your hearts to My mother. Be united as one in Our Hearts. Our Hearts are an endless abyss of love for you. Come to us. Find refuge in My most Sacred Heart.

I am Jesus. I am God. My Heart is burning for love of you. Constantly come to My Heart. I will give you peace.

Father, Fashion Me More into Your Child

R.Father, mold me, fashion me more into the little child You want me to be, the little child You created me to be. Fashion me more into Your child, to give love to this hurting world.

I am your Jesus, sweet one, fear not. I go with you. Your job will be easy, for what you do is My work. Your love for Me is all that matters to save the starved souls. You will help lead souls to eternal salvation. My letters will feed them, My food. You will feed the hungry.

I will be your Rear Guard and your Fore Guard. You will be molded into My special messenger of love. Teach others to live for Me. My command is to love Me first, and to love your neighbor as yourself.

I am Love. I will give love to the hurting souls. Spread the letters. Souls are at stake! I am Jesus and I have spoken. My kingdom awaits and it is not of this world. Forget your worldly attachments and come and dwell deep in My Heart. Father, forgive them, they know not what they do!

Your salvation is won through My Heart. My blood is spent. Heaven is a reward granted to those who love and serve the Lord. Come to Me, love Me, serve Me. You will minister to this, oh, so sick world. I am Jesus. You are My beloved ones. Love God, love one another. So simple? This is My children's priority. Teach them these things. I give you My letters. Feed this hungry world.

Love Your Hurting Brothers

My sweet one, the more you become intimate with Us, God, the Father, the Holy Spirit, and Me, the more you will love your brothers. You will see more and more the others and their needs and less and less of self.

The more you become intimate with Me, the more your needs are filled by Me and the more you can give to others.

A blind man does not see. You may not see the others and their pain. The more you pray to the Holy Spirit to see with the eyes of God, the more you see your brother and his needs. Two people may see a person in need. One will run to assist, the other will not even notice. It is the love of God within that causes you to see your hurting brothers.

You have so much to learn to be Christ-like. Pray to Me after Communion, pray to the Holy Spirit, read these letters. I will reveal such wisdom to you here. Oh, child, I love you so. Do not ever doubt. I will be always by your side. When you are weary, come to Me and I will give you rest.

I am the Lord, thy God. Thou shalt not have any gods before Me. This is My command to you. It is no little matter. I must be first in your life. Heaven is a reward promised to those who love and serve the Lord. Come to Me and I will give you rest.

R. And He came and they were filled with such love. Father, Son and Holy Spirit dwelt within their souls. They were filled and knew this promise. Alleluia.

Pains In the Heart

It is not that I love you and don't love your brothers. I loved them to My death. You must forgive, no matter how they have wronged you. See Me going to My death for them because I loved them. They are My Father's creation!

They ignored Me and they put Me to death. What did I do? You will suffer persecution. I am God. I know all things and they killed Me.

R. They hollered awful insults at Him and He didn't say a word.

The pains of the heart, My child! Only I have the love to sustain you. You must come to Me. Not to listen to My Will in the smallest thing will cause you such trouble.

Let them demand perfection. You are a human being. My letters are authentic. You, in all your imperfections, have nothing to do with the authenticity of My letters! You are under attack from all sides. It will get better, it will get worse. You will constantly fight this battle. You must surrender to My Will to remain selfless. You are a human. You sin, you err.

Nothing here that is worldly matters if it is not rooted in Me. Love one another as I have loved you. I showed you the way, you must follow Me. My way is the way to the Father. My way is the way to eternal life.

Be like Me in all your actions. I came, I showed you the way. You cannot straddle the fence. My way is the only way. It is the way of the cross.

Come to the recesses of My Heart and experience the love of God. Be united to Me and My mother in Our Hearts. Consecrate yourself to Me, My little ones. Consecrate your heart to My mother. Be united as one in Our Hearts. Our Hearts are an endless abyss of love for you. Come to Us. Find refuge in My most Sacred Heart.

I am Jesus. I am God. My Heart is burning for love of you. Constantly come to My Heart. I will give you peace.

June 30, 1994

Holy Spirit

R. Dear Spirit, oh, Holy Spirit, how little I tell You of my love! You are indeed a Person. You are God. It is through Your gifts that I receive the knowledge of God, to know, love and serve Him more. Open me, oh, Spirit. Open this closed heart of mine and fill me with the fire of Your love. Impart to me the tongues of fire I need to do the work God wants me to do. Give me Your love so I can love God more than myself. Help me to surrender to You and let You live and dwell in my heart in such union!

Oh, Spirit of God, open my eyes so I can see more and more with Your gifts what I need to see to serve and to love You. Help me to love my brothers as You want me to, to know how to love as God wants me to.

Mary, you are the spouse of the Holy Spirit. It is through Him that Jesus was conceived in your womb. Draw me to your Spouse, the Holy Spirit, to greater union with Him. Help me to love the Holy Spirit more and more through your Immaculate Heart.

Help me to grow in my intimacy with You, oh, Holy Spirit. Help me to hear what You want to tell me. You are the love between the Father and the Son. Help me to know the fire of this love. I want to know more Your love for me. I want to love You more, to grow in deeper union with You.

Mary, help me to love the Holy Spirit through your Immaculate Heart.

Father, Son, Holy Spirit: three Persons in one God. Each Person to be loved individually, yet God to be loved as One, in union with Mary! Such burning in my heart for each Person, a burning to love God, three in one, through Mary's Immaculate Heart.

I could spend such joyful hours dwelling on this immense love. God is present and truly in our midst and in our hearts. I cannot love my brothers as God wants me to if I do not know God. When I am filled with the love of God, then I can love my brothers as He wants: "that you are willing to lay down your life for your brother." It takes that intimacy, that oneness, to know God, to love as God wants me to love.

To love you, my brother, I must constantly try to be more united with the one, true, magnificent God. Through Mary, I learn to love God more intimately.

Open me, oh, Spirit of the living God. Open my heart to love, to the fire of Your love. Enkindle it deep in my heart. The love of the one, triune God!

Oh, Mary, help me to love God, Father, Son and Holy Spirit, through your Heart.

Praise God in His magnificence. Praise God, Father, Son and Holy Spirit! Let us pour out our abundant love, through Mary, on Them. Teach us to love You, God. Help us, in our littleness, to give You love through Mary's sinless Heart. I can grow in my intimacy with God, Father, Son and Holy Spirit.

Book Titles Available From Shepherds of Christ Publications

God's Blue Book, Volumes 1, 2 and 3, by Rita Ring. Lessons from Jesus about living in and loving Him in our times. Remarkable insights into appreciating Our Lord in the Blessed Sacrament and in the tabernacle. Private dialogues between God and a chosen one. Prayers of a soul carried by God to His heights.

Donation Price $5.00/vol.

Tell My People, messages as given to Father Edward J. Carter, S.J. from Jesus and Mary since April, 1994. Messages and reflections for growing in holiness through devotion to the Immaculate Heart of Mary and the Sacred Heart of Jesus.

Donation Price $4.00

Rosaries from the Hearts of Jesus and Mary, meditations and messages given by Jesus and Mary to Rita Ring during the praying of the Rosary. Includes instructions for praying the rosary, songs given by Jesus to be sung during the rosary, a complete set of 15 full-page pictures of the rosary windows at Our Lady of the Holy Spirit Center in Norwood, Ohio.

Donation Price $5.00

Rosary Mediations for Parents and Children, by Rita Ring. Short meditations (without messages) for both parents and children to be used when praying the rosary. These meditations will help all to know the lives of Jesus and Mary alive in their hearts.

Donation Price $5.00

The Spirituality of Fatima and Medjugorje, by Father Edward J. Carter, S.J. The key idea of this book is: "...We see the profound link, the profound point of convergence between the spirituality of Fatima and Medjugorje. It is the ongoing conversion based on consecration to the Sacred Heart and to the Immaculate Heart..." (page 43 of the text)

Donation Price $5.00

Mass Book, by Rita Ring. Journal entries of a chosen soul concerning the events during the Holy Sacrifice of the Mass. These entries help to lead other souls deeply into the Heart of Christ during the Mass.

Donation Price $7.00

Apostles Manual, (440 pages). A manual for Apostles in the Shepherds of Christ Movement.

Donation Price $7.50

Mother At My Side, by Fr. Edward J. Carter, S.J. An easy to read composite look at Mary's role in our lives. Fr. Carter incorporates this role with messages from Mary from around the world into all aspects of our spiritual journey through life.

Donation Price $6.00

General Order Form

For Any Shepherds of Christ Materials

Number
of Copies

☐ _____

☐ _____

☐ _____

☐ _____

☐ _____

☐ _____

☐ _____

☐ _____

☐ _____

☐ _____

☐ _____

☐ _____

☐ _____

☐ _____

☐ _____

☐ _____

Personal Mailing Address

Please print neatly. Thanks!

Name:

☐☐☐☐☐☐☐☐☐☐☐☐☐☐☐☐☐☐☐☐☐☐☐☐☐☐☐☐☐☐

Address:

☐☐☐☐☐☐☐☐☐☐☐☐☐☐☐☐☐☐☐☐☐☐☐☐☐☐☐☐☐☐

City   *State* *Zip Code*

☐☐☐☐☐☐☐☐☐☐☐☐☐☐☐ ☐☐☐ ☐☐☐☐☐-☐☐☐☐

Phone Number: (optional)

☐☐☐-☐☐☐-☐☐☐☐

I would like to be on the Shepherds of Christ mailing list. *yes* ☐ *no* ☐

Shepherds of Christ Publications is a subsidiary of Shepherds of Christ Ministries. Titles are available through religious bookstores or directly from the publisher:

Shepherds of Christ Publications
P.O. Box 193
Morrow, Ohio 45152

Shepherds of Christ Publications is the publishing arm of Shepherds of Christ Ministries, a non-profit corporation. Dedicated to fostering an increase in love of God and the Two Hearts, the Sacred Heart of Jesus and the Immaculate Heart of Mary, it supports its works entirely on donations such as those shown above. When ordering from the publisher, please add $1.50 for each book, total mailing cost not to exceed $10.00 per order. Audio tapes, video tapes and other printed materials are available. For more information about the ministries, especially the prayer chapters and publications for priests and religious, write to the above address, call Shepherds of Christ headquarters at 1-888-211-3041 or 1-513-932-4451; fax 1-513-932-6791.